GO ME

This book belongs to

TO CALLUM AND CHLOE,
MY LITTLE INSPIRATIONS FOR THIS BOOK! C.H.

First published 2020 by Walker Books Ltd
87 Vauxhall Walk, London SE11 5HJ

2 4 6 8 10 9 7 5 3 1

Text © 2020 Trackstars Ltd
Cover typography © 2020 Nic Farrell
Cover photograph © PA Images
Illustrations © 2020 Miguel Bustos
With thanks to consultant psychologist Professor Chris Harwood

This book has been typeset in Franklin Gothic

Printed in Italy

British Library Cataloguing in Publication Data:
a catalogue record for this book is available from the British Library

ISBN 978-1-4063-9473-3

www.walker.co.uk

WALKER BOOKS
AND SUBSIDIARIES
LONDON • BOSTON • SYDNEY • AUCKLAND

BE AMAZING!

CHRIS HOY

Contents

Hello!

My name is Chris Hoy and every day, for many years, I rode a bike as fast as I possibly could. There's a good chance you won't have heard of me, as I stopped racing back in 2013, but I did quite well competing for Great Britain on the velodrome as a track cyclist.

In total, I won six Olympic gold medals, eleven World Championship gold medals and thirty-four World Cup gold medals.

Typing that out now, I still find it completely bizarre... Me? An Olympic champion?! Not just once, but six times?! My ten-year-old self would have laughed out loud at how unbelievable that sounds!

*There's **NO WAY** that could **EVER** happen to me!* I would have thought back then. ***I'm not even the fastest kid on my street. How on earth could I even DREAM of being the best in the world at riding a bike?!***

I didn't set out to become a champion. I started riding a bike because of an alien (more on that later!) and I then carried on simply because I loved doing it. My bike was all I thought about, talked about, dreamed about. It was my passion.

I wasn't particularly good at it, though! Between the ages of six and sixteen, you certainly wouldn't have picked me out as a possible gold-medal winner, compared to some of the other much faster kids. I definitely didn't believe that I was a future champion, either.

So how did I go from being a kid on a BMX to living my dream as an adult, representing my country at world level? Well, that's what I'm going to tell you. I wrote this book to give you the inside scoop on my journey to becoming an Olympic champion, in the hope that you might be able to use these tips to achieve your dream – whatever it might be.

This is not a book about cycling. You don't need to be enthusiastic about bikes, the Olympics or even sport in general to read this book. (Although if you are obsessed with riding bikes really fast around a track, then brilliant!) I believe I've discovered things on my journey to a gold medal that apply to everyone.

This is also not a book that's about winning or learning how to win. I didn't want to write a guide to becoming the best in the world at something. Winning is absolutely not the most important thing in life, believe me when I say that.

Instead, this is a book all about

I want to help you discover the feeling of being your best – no matter what it is you love doing. It's a guide to becoming your own champion, discovering a dream and seeing how far you can go on your journey. You have way more potential than you think. I want you to surprise yourself and others!

Often when we see someone achieve something incredible on TV, they make it look effortless. Whether it's Usain Bolt running the 100 metres or Beyoncé singing the finale at a sell-out concert, they do it with such apparent ease you might think they aren't even trying and are just using their natural talents. But those performances are actually the result of years of hard work, determination, planning and practice – and a little bit of luck sprinkled on top. Becoming the best you can be takes time and effort, no matter who you are.

We all have dreams. We all have potential. Just think how exciting it would be to use your potential and make something amazing happen! Now how do you begin that journey? The good news is that you can start today, right now, by reading this guide.

Each chapter of this book is based around something important I learned on my journey to becoming an Olympic champion. I hope each chapter will help you to follow your dream, whatever it may be – whether it is playing for your favourite team, becoming a chef or mastering a skateboard trick.

I believe this guide will give you the tools to go out there and begin your journey, and to have the confidence to try your best and not worry about the outcome. But most of all, I want it to inspire you to find something that you love and enjoy.

Over the years, I've been lucky enough to meet many incredible and unique people from all around the world who have achieved great things in sport, music, acting, singing, art, writing, cooking, dance, business, comedy, broadcasting, technology and so on. Some of their amazing stories feature in this book.

The majority of them, when asked about how they began their journey, say the same thing: it started out as a passion and they kept at it because they loved it. Very few felt that it was their destiny, or that they always believed that they would succeed. They weren't extraordinary and they didn't have superpowers that guaranteed their success. Everyone starts from somewhere and was once just like you or me.

Just think that today could be the first step on your new adventure. It could lead you anywhere you want to go! The sooner you start reading, the sooner you can begin. The more you put into your journey, the more you will get out, so throw yourself at it, be positive and give it a go.

And have fun!

Chapter 1

GET INSPIRED

FIND SOMETHING THAT MAKES YOU FEEL AMAZING

Where champions begin

This chapter is all about beginnings.
I want you to know right at the start of your journey
something that took me many years to learn.

I used to think that Olympic champions were different to the rest of us. They were born to be great and their success or talent came naturally to them. I could never have imagined them doing everyday things like school and homework or going to the dentist. But the more I saw during my time in the Great Britain cycling team, the more I realized that champions in sport – and in life in general – are just normal people who commit themselves to one thing and work incredibly hard at it. They push themselves every day to be the very best they can be, but at the heart of it is the fact that they enjoy what they do. I now believe that becoming your own champion begins with finding something you love doing.

I bet your life is similar to mine when I was your age. You go to school and mess around with your friends. I loved riding my bike and playing rugby, but maybe you play football instead, or dance, swim, play the guitar or bake. Have you already found an activity you really enjoy? If so, great! We're going to discover how you can become the best you can be at it. If not, don't worry! Inspiration can come from the most unlikely of places and we are going to look at where you can find it.

My cycling story began when I was a kid and ***spoiler alert*** it involved an alien. After some twists and turns, and years of hard work, my journey led me somewhere very exciting: the Athens 2004 Olympic Games, where I was in the running to become Olympic champion for the first time.

Let me tell you how it felt to be there. If I can do it, then so can YOU!

We call to the start line the final competitor. From Great Britain: Chris Hoy!

I'm inside the velodrome, waiting on the start line for the 1,000-metre time trial at the Athens 2004 Olympic Games. The August evening is sweltering and I'm also feeling the heat.

My bike is locked into position in the start gate. I stare out at the familiar sight. I've cycled around a banked wooden track just like this thousands of times before. But today is different. Today is my chance to turn a dream I've had since I was fourteen into a reality. Four laps of this track lie between me and a gold medal.

I'm the final competitor. All the other cyclists from around the world have ridden and set their best times. They have been so fast that the Olympic record has been broken three times in the last five minutes. Now it is my turn. All I have to do is cycle as fast as I can against the clock. In those four laps, I need to show the world what I can do. This is my chance...

I take one last deep breath and lean forwards to grip my handlebars. In just over one minute's time, I could be an Olympic champion.

I'm ready.

But before I tell you what happened in the next sixty seconds, I want to stop and look back at what happened in the hours, days, weeks, months and years that led to this incredible moment.

How did I go from being a scrawny kid in Edinburgh who loved mucking around on his BMX, to an athlete representing his country at the biggest sporting event on the planet? I wasn't born naturally talented at cycling – no one is! What made me want to work for years and years towards this one massive goal? Where did my amazing journey begin?

Well, it all began with a moment of inspiration when I was six.

DING!

What is inspiration?

Inspiration happens when you see or experience something that makes you want to try it for yourself. Seeing what others have achieved gives us all something to aim for – and hopefully one day surpass. Inspiration is what keeps pushing the human race forwards: whether it's in science, technology, music, art or even, in my case, riding a bike as fast as possible!

When Andy Murray won Wimbledon, thousands of people across the country started turning up at local tennis clubs wanting to play.

Sales of baking equipment have rocketed in the UK with the popularity of the TV show The Great British Bake Off.

When England's netball team beat the world champions Australia in the final of the 2018 Commonwealth Games, there was a 44 per cent increase in participation the following year.

The chances are that you've already been inspired to try something new many times in your life – probably without even realizing it.

Have you ever wanted to try something you've seen an older brother or sister, your mum or dad or a friend doing?

Have you ever tried doing something you've seen online or on TV, or that you've read about in a book or a magazine?

Have you been inspired by something you've seen while walking down the street? Or had an exciting thought come to you while brushing your teeth?

Inspiration can come from anyone, anywhere, at any time. You just have to be ready to act on it – because it can change everything!

Sometimes, you can search for inspiration without any success. Other times, it pops up out of the blue and surprises you.

An alien changed my life

When I was six, I watched a film called *E.T.* about an extraterrestrial who is trying to find his way back to his home planet. The alien didn't inspire me to become an astronomer, and the performances didn't make me want to try acting. However, I did see a BMX bike for the first time.

There's a great scene where a group of kids on BMXs are chased by the police. They take air over jumps, do wheelies and carve through corners. It looked like a huge amount of fun and I wanted to have a go, so I asked my mum and dad for a BMX for Christmas.

BMXs had only just arrived in the UK from America and were very expensive. I already had a bike, which I loved, that had cost £5 at a local jumble sale. My parents thought my sudden interest was just a passing craze, so rather than buy a new bike, my dad changed the handlebars and grips on my regular bike, sprayed it black and covered it in BMX stickers.

When I unwrapped it on Christmas day, I was blown away. I had my very own BMX! (Well, sort of…) I knew it wasn't the real thing, but it meant that I could now get outside and practise the moves I'd seen in *E.T.* And once I started riding my "BMX", I didn't want to stop. I had found a lifelong passion for cycling that continues to this day. Every time I get on a bike, I want to be the very best I can be.

Time flies when you're having fun

Before long, all I could think about was riding my BMX. I would stay out on it for hours and hours every weekend until I was physically exhausted, only going inside the house to grab a drink or something to eat! I was having a great time and the hours I was putting in meant my bike-handling skills were improving. Soon I could do some of the moves from *E.T.* Not too much longer after that, I started racing every weekend at my local BMX track.

If you love doing something, you are more likely to push yourself to be the best you can be. You've probably noticed that some lessons at school seem to drag on for ever, while others – the ones that you enjoy – come to an end before you know it. That same principle applies here and it is a win–win situation. If you can find something you really love, not only will you have a great time doing it, you are also much more likely to become amazing at it!

When you enjoy what you do, you work harder at it without even realizing it. And if you're working harder, you will be more likely to improve.

The power of POSITIVE

You are unlikely to be inspired if you have a negative attitude. If you tell yourself that you won't enjoy something, that you're unlikely to get selected, that you never win things or that you're not the sort of person who picks up new skills quickly, then you will limit what you can do – before you've even had a go.

Throw yourself into every opportunity, keep smiling and see what happens!

How to get **inspired**

So, now you're thinking positively, what does this mean for you? I want you to think about things you love so much you could do them for hours on end. It could be sport, music, dance, cooking, art, writing, drama, vlogging or stargazing – anything that you enjoy.

WRITE DOWN THREE ACTIVITIES THAT MAKE YOU WANT TO THROW DOWN THIS BOOK AND GO AND DO THEM RIGHT NOW.

Don't worry if you can't immediately think of something that inspires you. I was very lucky to find cycling when I was six. Often it takes a while and you may have to try lots of activities before you discover the one that's just right for you.

The important thing is that you open your eyes to the world around you. It can be tempting to just do sports, subjects or clubs you already like and not bother trying new ones, worried that you won't be good at them or won't enjoy them. But everyone starts somewhere and you won't know unless you give it a go.

 You might love sport and think that's all you want to do, but the next time there's an audition for a school play, why not give it a try? It could be fun!

You might think that sport isn't for you. You've tried football, hockey, rugby and tennis but didn't really enjoy them. But there are hundreds of different sports out there that appeal to different sorts of personalities. You might prefer an individual sport like cycling, athletics or swimming, rather than a team sport. Or something like snooker, archery or golf that requires skill and precision more than huge physical exertion.

You might want to try something new but are holding back because none of your friends are interested in it. Well, at the end of the day, inspiration is all about how you feel, so you should try it anyway.

Say YES to new activities, even if they seem scary, silly or simply not for you. The more you try, the greater chance you have of being inspired and finding something that can become your passion. Just because you haven't found anything that you enjoy just yet doesn't mean that there isn't something waiting for you in the years ahead.

WRITE DOWN THREE NEW ACTIVITIES THAT YOU'VE NEVER DONE BEFORE. MAKE A PLAN TO TRY THEM WITHIN A TIME LIMIT SUCH AS A WEEK OR A MONTH.

Believe in **yourself**

When you are looking for inspiration, don't let others put you off trying something new. Sometimes people tell you what they think you're good at and what they think you're bad at. Or they put words in your mouth and say you like or dislike certain things. Being categorized like this is known as being pigeonholed.

No female jockey has ever won a Grade 1 race!

He's good at schoolwork, but he's not very sporty!

You can't be in the musical — your singing is terrible!

She's no good at maths — she should stick to less science-based subjects!

You're too short to play basketball — you'll never manage against the taller players!

Formula 1 is a man's sport. You'll never make it as a racing driver!

It's very easy to listen to people when they say things like this, especially if they are a friend, teacher or family member. But other people aren't always right! What inspires you might not be the same thing that your friends or family get excited about, but that doesn't mean it's not worth pursuing. And if no one from your family or school has done it before, well, it's even more of a reason to have a go!

Don't let other people knock your confidence or talk you out of it. Stay positive! If you are enjoying yourself, then, right now, that's the number-one most important thing. The chances of you sticking with that activity as you get older will be so much higher if you do.

Leave your comfort zone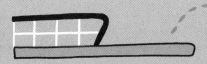

Sometimes it can be a bit daunting – or even plain scary – to try something that pushes you out of your comfort zone. Have you ever had the feeling of butterflies in your stomach when you're asked to read in front of the whole class? Or when you're standing on the start line of a 100-metre race? Or when you're waiting backstage for your first entrance in a play? Don't worry – that feeling is totally normal!

There have been many moments in my life when I've been really nervous about going out of my comfort zone. Even when I was making tiny BMX ramps in my back garden with planks of wood and bricks, I remember how terrified and excited I felt when I pedalled flat out towards the ramp. I was probably only getting my wheels a few centimetres off the ground, but the rush I felt afterwards from having done something I hadn't done before made me want to do it again! Later, I experienced the exact same feeling at races when I competed for the first time at a new level or in front of a big crowd.

Feeling nervous is often your body and brain's way of telling you that you are taking a step into the unknown. You don't quite know what is going to happen next. But don't be put off by that feeling. Those butterflies in your stomach are a good sign. They show that you are challenging yourself. Use your nerves to focus your mind and give your new experience your absolute all.

Be inspired to be YOUR best

When you start a new activity, try not to focus on whether you are good or bad at it. That applies to anything from hockey to skateboarding or singing in a choir. Most people aren't immediately great at sport, schoolwork, art, dancing or music. Even if you're having fun, it still takes time and practice to get better at everything.

When I started BMX racing, I wasn't particularly good at it. Most of the time I would come somewhere in the middle. Sometimes I would finish second or third and I would go home with a medal (I've still got them all in a box at home). Sometimes I would crash and finish last. In fact, one time I crashed, got back on my bike and then crashed again before I made it to the finish line!

You don't have to be the best, but just keep trying *your* best. Try not to get hung up on where you are compared to your friends' achievements. It's very tempting to give up if you tell yourself you will never be as good as the people around you. Instead, learn from

others. I used to be quite good at watching the older kids at BMX races, studying how they went over the jumps or the lines they took through the corners, and then copying the moves myself. Slowly, at my own pace, I improved. Once in a while, I would even win a race!

Even so, I wouldn't have been picked out as a future Olympic champion at the age of ten. There were loads of other kids my age who were faster or showed more potential. I certainly never would have believed that I would become the best in the world at anything. Why would I? I was good at sport, but not great. I did fine in school, but I wasn't top of the class.

We all grow, develop, learn and improve at different rates. My story shows that just because you're not the best at something now, you can still be amazing at it when you're older. The world is full of people who have worked hard to become incredible at what they do, but that doesn't mean that they were brilliant at it to begin with. You have the potential to do more than you can ever imagine.

Let me finish telling you about the Athens 2004 Olympics, because there is no way ten-year-old me would have thought that could happen to him. Let's go back to the velodrome and that start line. I'm about to ride the most important four laps of my life.

You want to know what happened, right?!

Going for gold
The countdown beeps start and I grip my handlebars even more tightly …
5, 4, 3, 2, 1 … GO!

I launch myself out of the starting gate, pushing down on the left pedal and pulling up on the right pedal with every bit of energy I have in my body. I attack the first lap, accelerating to maximum speed and then settle into a rhythm, my legs spinning round and round in a blur.

All I can hear from inside my pointy aerodynamic helmet is the roar of the crowd. I can't hear the commentator's voice over the loudspeakers and I can't hear my family screaming from the stands.

I have spent years dreaming of this moment and now here it is. Somehow I have gone from being a kid watching a film about an alien to an adult representing his country at the highest level, trying to win the unthinkable: an Olympic gold medal.

But there's no time to dwell on this thought. I have to keep pushing on. As I hurtle around each banked corner of the track my bike leans over. The sensation is incredible – it feels like I'm flying.

I cross the line at the end of my first lap. My time appears on the scoreboard for the crowd to see and there's a huge roar. I can't look because I'm too focused on following the quickest route around the velodrome.

For a moment I think that it's a good sign that the crowd are cheering loudly. "I must be ahead," I tell myself. But then I think perhaps the noise is from fans delighted that I'm falling behind the time set by the previous French rider. The cheers might not be for me! I'd better push on...

The second lap is where the pain starts to really build in my legs and lungs. The effort needed to get up to speed is so great that very shortly afterwards there's a stinging sensation in my muscles which becomes less and less bearable. I'm trying to maintain my speed and keep the rhythm but it's getting harder and harder to do so. I cross the line at the end of the second lap. The crowd gives another loud ROAR.

It's lap three now and I'm past the halfway point. The temptation is to put too much effort in, to launch the sprint for the finish line, but it's too far away still. If I push too hard at this stage I will run out of steam. "Keep spinning, keep spinning," I tell myself. "You're going to hear the bell for the last lap very soon..."

I cross the line and there is another **ROAR**.

THE FINAL LAP! As I enter the home straight, I hear the

CLANG, CLANG, CLANG

of the bell above the yells from the thousands of spectators. The pain in my muscles is agony now. I'm trying to hang on, wringing every last drop of power out as I head towards the finish line.

But I can feel my pace slow. No, I can't give up!

I start to move around more on the bike, leaning from side to side with each turn of my pedals, losing my smooth technique, trying to summon any energy from within. I know winning this race is going to come down to fractions of a second. The finish line is so close now…

I put my head down and drive for the end, one last surge with everything I have. I lunge for the finish, stretching my arms out to push the bike at the line. It's over.

There's a split second where it seems like everyone in the velodrome turns to look at the scoreboard to see my final time and overall position.

And then …

ROOOOAAAAAAAAAAARRRRRR!!!!!!

The velodrome roof felt like it was going to lift off with the noise the crowd was making. I turned up to the scoreboard and saw it:

1ST CHRIS HOY GBR 1 MIN 00.711 SEC
NEW OLYMPIC RECORD

I'd done it! I'd become an Olympic champion. Me, Chris! That kid who had watched *E.T.* twenty-two years before. I was in shock.

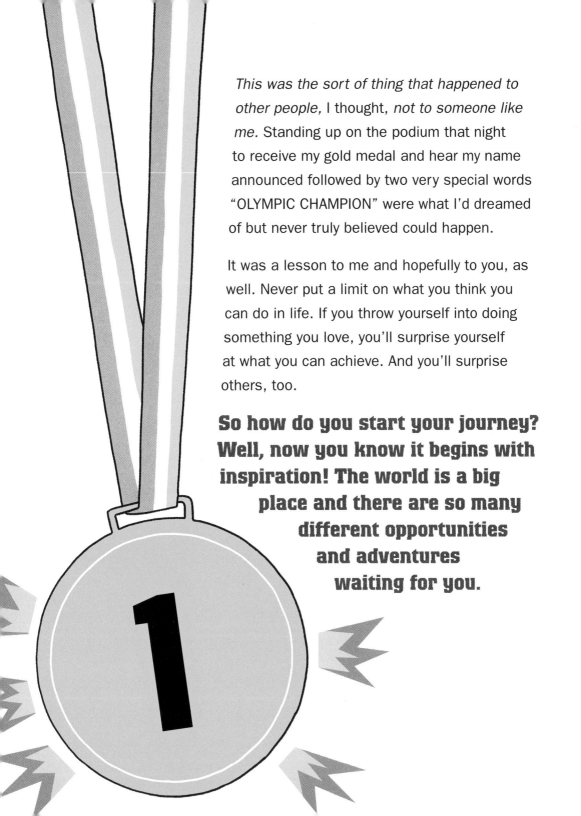

This was the sort of thing that happened to other people, I thought, *not to someone like me.* Standing up on the podium that night to receive my gold medal and hear my name announced followed by two very special words "OLYMPIC CHAMPION" were what I'd dreamed of but never truly believed could happen.

It was a lesson to me and hopefully to you, as well. Never put a limit on what you think you can do in life. If you throw yourself into doing something you love, you'll surprise yourself at what you can achieve. And you'll surprise others, too.

So how do you start your journey? Well, now you know it begins with inspiration! The world is a big place and there are so many different opportunities and adventures waiting for you.

Chapter 2
DARE TO DREAM
BELIEVE IN YOURSELF AND AIM FOR AMAZING

Achieving the impossible

You've been inspired. You've found something that you love doing and now you can't get enough of it. Excellent! So what's the next step in your journey to becoming your own champion? The previous chapter involved an alien and this one involves heroes!

It's time to sit back, relax and dare to dream. What do you imagine yourself achieving one day? Do you dream of being like one of your heroes? This part of your journey is all about aiming as high as you possibly can. Someone has to achieve the impossible – so why can't that person be you?!

Your amazing daydreams

Do you ever find yourself daydreaming in class, in the car or at the table? Maybe you are in the middle of doing something you do every day – such as eating breakfast – but your brain

is somewhere far away. In your daydream, you are doing something far more exciting than having a bowl of cereal!

The fun thing about daydreaming is that you can imagine yourself in all sorts of incredible situations, doing things way beyond what you can do right now. My daydreams included:

SCORING THE WINNING TRY FOR SCOTLAND IN THE CALCUTTA CUP

LANDING A 720 ON A SKATEBOARD HALF-PIPE

DRIVING A RALLY CAR FLAT OUT THROUGH THE FOREST STAGE OF THE WORLD RALLY CHAMPIONSHIP

WINNING AN OLYMPIC GOLD MEDAL IN CYCLING

My dreams were so real that I could hear cheers from the crowd as I scored the winning try and see the mud splattering my windscreen in the World Rally Championship.

But far from being pointless or time-wasting, your daydreams can motivate you. Your imagination is a very powerful force.

LET YOUR IMAGINATION WANDER...

Imagine what it must be like to walk onstage to play in the headline band on the main stage at Glastonbury Festival, to see the tens of thousands of faces jumping up and down, clapping and cheering as you start your first song!

Imagine stepping up, as captain of the team, to take the last penalty kick in a shoot-out at the World Cup final, feeling the nerves, the excitement, the noise, the anticipation from the crowd as you are about to win — or lose — the cup for your country!

Imagine flying high in the sky as the pilot of a fighter jet, travelling faster than the speed of sound, doing acrobatic manoeuvres and feeling the G-forces squeezing your body as you change direction!

You can imagine ANYTHING you want!

Think about what inspires you and what you really love doing.

CLOSE YOUR EYES NOW AND IMAGINE AN INCREDIBLE THING YOU DREAM OF DOING ONE DAY. TRY AND MAKE YOUR DAYDREAM AS REAL AS POSSIBLE, SO CAPTURE ALL THE DETAILS OF WHAT YOU SEE, HEAR AND SMELL, AND ALSO HOW YOU FEEL.

When you are daydreaming, take control of the story and imagine you are directing yourself in the movie of your ultimate life. You are the star actor! You are watching yourself right in the action, successfully completing each and every task. The more you mentally practise and replay this movie in your mind, the more your brain becomes familiar with the experience. This lays down the foundation for developing, learning and producing these skills in real life.

Your
amazing
heroes

Don't worry if you can't immediately think of something incredible to daydream about. Think instead about someone who inspires you. Who do you look up to – and why? I've had many heroes in my life and they all helped shape my dreams and goals.

Gavin Hastings was the captain of the Scotland international rugby team when I was a kid, and he was the person who I was thinking of when I was dreaming of scoring in the Calcutta Cup. I used to watch his matches, trying to learn how to be more like him. He scored match-winning tries and was also the kicker with the responsibility of taking crucial conversions and penalties.

One Tuesday after our school rugby practice, when I was ten, our coach made an announcement:

We are very lucky to have an extremely special guest joining us for today's training session. Everybody, give a big welcome to the Scotland captain, GAVIN HASTINGS!

I was so excited! "Big Gav" watched us train and gave us some tips. We all put in that little bit of extra effort, hoping to impress him. He then talked about how he started playing rugby at school, and how he dreamed of playing for Scotland one day. He hadn't thought that it would ever happen, but he worked hard and didn't give up. One day his dream came true. He said the same thing could happen to us!

Until that point, I'd never thought that someone like him – one of my greatest heroes – might have once been a kid like me, playing rugby at school. It blew my mind to discover that he might have had to work really hard to get where he was in his sport. It was so motivating to realize that an ordinary kid like me could, in theory, become captain of Scotland if I wanted it enough.

WHO DO YOU DREAM OF BEING LIKE ONE DAY? WHAT ACTIONS HAVE MADE THAT PERSON YOUR HERO? WRITE DOWN THE ATTRIBUTES THAT YOU ADMIRE ABOUT THEM, SUCH AS BEING A GOOD TEAM PLAYER OR A MOTIVATING CAPTAIN. THINK ABOUT WHETHER YOU SHARE ANY OF THOSE QUALITIES.

Every hero starts somewhere

When you are daydreaming and imagining that one day you could become one of your heroes, it's easy to think that they were born successful or that their success has happened overnight, as if by magic. You might therefore think that you have no chance of really being like them.

Always remember: YOUR HEROES AREN'T SUPERHUMAN!

What they have achieved through years and years of practice can seem superhuman, but they themselves aren't. **They are just like you and me!**

Our heroes are normal people who have dedicated their lives to their dreams. They've stuck with those dreams, even when it seemed like it might be impossible to achieve them. When you and I watch them from our sofas, we are left open-mouthed in awe at their abilities. But they haven't always been able to perform like that. They discovered something they enjoyed doing and became good at it because they did it again and again and again.

They grew from kids with dreams into the heroes that they are today. They set themselves goals so they would keep improving until they had reached their very best. They took criticism and failure and didn't let it get them down. Instead, they used the feedback to help them come back better and stronger.

Realizing your heroes aren't superhuman shouldn't shatter an illusion. Knowing that they are ordinary people should make them even more incredible, because you can now see that being amazing is within your grasp if you set yourself careful goals.

My BIGGEST hero

Graeme Obree, the world champion cyclist, smashed the world hour record twice (the furthest distance a person can cover in an hour on a velodrome track). Not only did he break one of the most significant records in cycling, he did it without a support team on a home-made bicycle built from scrap metal and old washing-machine parts!

Obree worked incredibly hard physically, but he also pushed himself mentally. Instead of worrying about other people's expectations, he set himself huge goals and took them on in his own way. He questioned everything, looking for new ideas or techniques. He even invented a new riding position, where he tucked his arms in close to his chest to make himself as fast as possible.

To me, Obree was the ultimate superhero. But when I met him, I realized he was an ordinary person driven to do something extraordinary because he was passionate about it. He didn't think he was special; he just wanted to achieve his goal so much he was prepared to give it his absolute all. His determination inspired me to aim as high as I possibly could.

"My biggest fear isn't crashing this bike at 85mph and losing my skin. It's sitting in a chair at ninety and thinking, 'I wish I'd done more.'"

GRAEME OBREE

No dream is impossible

Someone had to be the first person to climb Mount Everest, walk on the Moon, run a marathon in under two hours or do a double wheelchair backflip. And all along the way the people who achieved those firsts would have been told that their dreams were impossible. But records are broken, rankings change and people go further and faster. Never think that your dream is impossible or that you can't match the feats of your hero.

Someone has to achieve your dream, so why not YOU?

A daydream is usually something that stays in your head and is fun to think about when your mind is wandering in the middle of a maths lesson. So let's look at getting it out of your head and turning it into a reality.

WRITE YOUR DREAM DOWN ON A PIECE OF PAPER RIGHT NOW. IT SHOULD BE SOMETHING HUGE, SOMETHING MASSIVE, SOMETHING THAT MIGHT EVEN SEEM RIDICULOUS TO YOU AT THIS MOMENT IN TIME!

My HUGE, MASSIVE, RIDICULOUS dream is
....

Doing this shouldn't make you feel like you are under any kind of pressure. You can write your dream down and not show it to anyone else if you don't want to.

NOW WRITE DOWN THE EMOTIONS YOU THINK YOU WOULD EXPERIENCE IF YOU ACHIEVED YOUR RIDICULOUS DREAM.

I bet you'd feel pretty amazing, right?! So wouldn't you rather have a go at achieving your dream – and experiencing that feeling – than just spending the rest of your life imagining what it would be like?

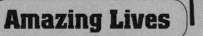

The rally car driver who achieved the impossible

Bartosz Ostałowski is a rally car driver who competes professionally in different motorsport events. When he was nineteen, he lost both of his arms in a motorbike accident. He was determined not to give up on his dream of becoming a champion driver, but he was told again and again that it was impossible. No one had ever driven a car competitively without their arms.

> *"My next step should be more wins. Like any driver, I'd like to win the championship."*
> BARTOSZ OSTAŁOWSKI

Rather than giving up, Ostałowski worked on his flexibility, strength and coordination. He adapted his car with his mechanics and engineers. Together they created a vehicle that he could drive using only his feet and shoulders. The footage of him competing is astonishing! His left foot controls the steering wheel, his right foot operates the brake, throttle, accelerator and handbrake, and he uses his shoulders to change gear.

Ostałowski proved that his dream wasn't impossible. It was just that no one had done it before. His story shows what ambition and determination can achieve.

The young boxer with a BIG dream

Nicola Adams, a professional boxer, has been European, World, Commonwealth and Olympic champion. When she was a kid, she kept telling her friends and family about her dream to compete at the Olympics. Their response was: "Nicola, women's boxing isn't even an Olympic sport!"

But Adams refused to take that as an answer. She told her family that women's boxing would one day become an Olympic sport and that she was going to compete in it. She also told them that she was going to win a gold medal. In the end, she became the first female boxer to win an Olympic gold medal at the London 2012 Games. In fact, she proved her family wrong a second time, by going on to win gold in the Rio 2016 Olympics.

"I was thirteen when I decided I was going to win an Olympic gold medal."
NICOLA ADAMS

My (im)possible dream

When I was fourteen, and a member of my local cycling club in Edinburgh, our coach asked us each to write down our ultimate dream of what we would like to achieve in cycling.

Now, just so you know, I wasn't the best junior rider in Britain at that time. I wasn't the best in Scotland or in Edinburgh. I wasn't even the best rider in the room! But I decided that if I had the chance to dream, then I was going HUGE! So I wrote down:

GOLD MEDAL IN THE 2004 OLYMPIC GAMES 1,000-METRE TIME TRIAL

We then had to read out what we'd written. There were about twelve of us in the junior section of the club. As we went round the group, one by one, I realized that I was the only one to aim for such a ridiculously high target. My friends had written things like:

REPRESENT SCOTLAND AT THE COMMONWEALTH GAMES.

REPRESENT GB AT THE OLYMPIC GAMES.

WIN A MEDAL FOR SCOTLAND AT THE COMMONWEALTH GAMES.

RIDE IN THE TOUR DE FRANCE.

These were all fantastic dreams and very big challenges indeed. But none of my friends were aiming as high as they possibly could. No one was dreaming of going all the way to be their *very* best. That might have been for lots of different reasons: they might have felt that they couldn't do it, or there were other people who were more talented than them – or simply that their dream was so unlikely to come true, it wasn't worth writing down.

I was lucky to have a supportive coach. When I read out my dream, he didn't laugh or tell me that winning a gold medal was impossible for me. Instead, he said:

"If you want to achieve your dream, you need to start by turning it into a goal."

This was some of the best advice I've ever been given because it gave me a way to turn that incredible moment in my imagination into a reality. Suddenly it felt like I had a map that would guide me on the journey I would need to take if I was going to become an Olympic champion.

Believe in your dream and believe in yourself. With positive thinking and careful planning, you can turn your big dream into smaller, more achievable goals. You have nothing to lose, so commit to your dream and see how many of those goals you can hit!

Small steps towards a **BIG** dream

Now the idea of goal-setting might sound a bit serious, the sort of thing that could take the fun out of your dream, but having a goal gives you the focus you need to take on bigger and bigger challenges.

After I had decided that my dream was to become Olympic champion in 2004, my coach encouraged me to identify short-term mini-goals that would act as stepping stones towards the big one. My first three were as follows:

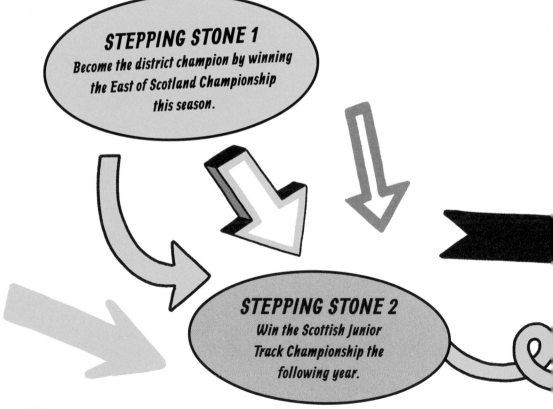

STEPPING STONE 1
Become the district champion by winning the East of Scotland Championship this season.

STEPPING STONE 2
Win the Scottish Junior Track Championship the following year.

Once I had each stepping stone clear in my mind, I then planned the detailed training I would need to follow to hit these targets. We'll look at how to plan and practise in Chapter 4.

When turning your dream into smaller goals, make sure those goals are within your grasp to achieve within a certain length of time. So, for example, if your dream is to one day swim the Channel, start building up your distances gradually. Your first stepping stone could be for 750 metres and you can build up until you can swim 5,000 metres in six months' time. Once you have hit that stepping stone, you can aim for the next one, and then the next one after that. If you keep doing this, it'll eventually lead you to your ultimate dream.

It's within your grasp to achieve all kinds of amazing goals. Yes, you will need support, guidance, coaching and a bit of luck to make it from stepping stone to stepping stone. These things may not all appear to be readily available to you right now, but if you are brave, aim high and begin your journey with the right attitude, you'll be surprised how many people want to join you for the ride and help you along the way.

STEPPING STONE 3
Be selected for the Great Britain under-23 squad the year after that.

Reality check

Before you begin chasing your dream, there are five important things I want you to remember.

1. Be prepared to work *very* hard

If what you are trying to achieve was easy, then everyone would be doing it – and brilliantly, at that! Ultimately, your motivation has to come from within you. You can't rely on a coach, teacher, parent or friend to push you forwards to being your best. You need the fire in your belly! Luckily, that's not actual flames, but the feeling of being driven to aim high for its own sake.

2. Expect highs and lows

Don't expect things to go to plan. Sometimes they will and you will feel on top of the world. But you'll experience bumps along the way, and, believe me, it'll be incredibly frustrating. The setbacks and disappointments are all part of the process.

3. Don't make it all about the goal

When you see the runners lining up at the start of the 100 metres Olympic final, you are looking at eight exceptional athletes. Only one gets to win gold. Why would those athletes want to give their absolute all for years and years to something that might not work out? The answer is simple: BECAUSE IT'S FUN! It isn't just about the medal or the end result; it's about the journey. Enjoy what you do simply for the sake of doing it and you will go further as a result.

4. Success is never guaranteed

Even if you aim high, work hard and don't give up when it gets tough, there's still no guarantee of success. But don't see this as a negative. You might not achieve what you set out to do, but if you've given it your absolute all, then that's OK. In fact, it's more than OK – what you've done is amazing! You've found your personal best and you should be extremely proud of yourself.

5. Have a Plan B

The honest truth is that only a very, very small percentage of people will get to be the very best in the world and achieve the sort of huge goal that I hope you are aiming for. That doesn't mean you shouldn't aim for it – of course not! Someone has to achieve it, so why not you? But it is worth having a Plan B that will take away any pressure or worry you might feel around not achieving it. Let me tell you about my Plan B.

When I was in my late teens, there wasn't a clear route for me to become a professional cyclist. There were no places to train in the winter, no full-time coaches and zero funding. And the biggest challenge of all was that I wasn't even that good. My Olympic goal was enormous! My parents said that I had to have a back-up plan. I decided that a university degree would be good to fall back on. I worked hard, got reasonable grades and a place. When I was there, my studies took priority, even though I still trained hard. Once I graduated, I knew it was now the time to give my goal my all and see how far I could go.

AIM FOR THE STARS AND YOU MIGHT HIT THE MOON INSTEAD

One of the best things about aiming as high as you possibly can is that if you get close to your dream, but don't quite hit it, you'll still have done something amazing and very possibly way beyond what you ever thought you'd be capable of! Your experiences might lead to other opportunities that you had never even imagined in the first place.

Jon Norfolk's story is a great example of this. He was a member of the Great Britain cycling squad and his dream was to make the Olympic team and win a gold medal. He worked incredibly hard in every session, followed his coach's training programme, had a positive attitude and did everything he possibly could to achieve his goal.

He never quite achieved his ultimate ambition, but he still represented his country, won national and international medals and travelled the world doing what he loved. He gained so much expertise and experience during his time competing and most importantly, never lost his passion for cycling. When he retired, he decided to start coaching. He went on to become the head coach for Great Britain's Paralympic team, was awarded an

MBE by the Queen and is now a senior coach for the Australian Olympic cycling team. That's an amazing set of achievements, even if they weren't the ones he had started out aiming for at the beginning.

What I learned from Jon is that if you have a positive attitude and keep doing your best, even if you don't hit your original target, you can still do incredible things.

So, go on ...
I dare you!

Have a dream, but never forget that the reason for having one is to challenge yourself to see what you're capable of. It's not about anyone else and if you don't achieve it, it's not the end of the world. You will have had a lot of fun in the process and become more confident and learned new skills. But you never know, you might do it, and wouldn't that be

AMAZING?

Chapter 3
FEEL POSITIVE
A CHANGE IN ATTITUDE CAN HAVE AMAZING RESULTS

It's in the mind

You've been inspired and found something you love doing. You also want to get better at it and you've boldly set an ambitious goal to work towards. So far, so amazing! Now how do you turn the dream in your head into a reality?

Achieving a dream isn't easy – if it was, everyone would be doing it! You are going to have great times, but also face some pretty steep challenges. What can you do to make it easier?

Let's start off by working out what you need in order to achieve your goal. What do you think is the single most important quality you have to have in order to be successful at what you've chosen to do? Let me have a guess that you're thinking:

I NEED TO BE GOOD AT MATHS TO UNDERSTAND CODING!

I NEED TO BE TALL TO BE A BASKETBALL PLAYER!

All of these are important skills and attributes, but right now, none of them are essential to becoming a basketball player, a singer, a cyclist, a coder or a gymnast.

But there's one quality that you do need if you are going to get the best out of yourself. We touched on it in the previous chapter and it's absolutely essential for achieving any of these dreams – in fact, if you can master it, it will become your superpower. You need to have a positive attitude.

Amazing potential

Forget about what you *think* you need to be able to do in order to hit your goal. Let go of words such as **talent**, **skill** or **ability**. Instead focus on something we all have heaps of:

POTENTIAL.

The amazing thing about potential is that every single one of us is able to grow, develop and improve at virtually anything at all. You have the potential to do incredible things.*

*There is a BUT, though.

To unlock your full potential and truly be the best you can be, you need to approach your goal with the right mindset.

We all chase dreams from different starting points. Some people have a head start in achieving their goal, whereas others are at a disadvantage. I was lucky. I had support from my family. Not everyone has that, though, or can afford to chase a dream.

You can't change how you start off, but you can change where you're heading. The right attitude is essential to this. Staying positive, showing your passion and putting everything you have into what you do will make other people more likely to help and support you. Positivity is infectious!

Positive power

Anthony Joshua, the Olympic gold medallist and professional heavyweight boxing champion of the world, is someone who has demonstrated how a positive attitude can change your life.

Joshua found himself on the wrong side of the law and facing time in prison, but used boxing as a way to get himself onto a different path in life. By giving his full focus to achieving his goals, he changed direction. His attitude and dedication show just how far you can go, regardless of where you begin.

"From the neck up is where you win or lose the battle... You have to lock yourself in and strategize your mindset."
ANTHONY JOSHUA

Finding the **positive**

To me, at its most basic level, having a positive attitude means being able to look for the good, not the bad. It's being able to focus on the things that you can do to improve a situation, rather than getting hung up on the things you can't.

When everything is going well, it can be quite easy to be positive. The sun is shining, you've got a good mark in a test and you won your last match – yay! Of course you feel happy.

The real challenge is to be positive when you feel things aren't going your way. Part of that process is learning how to cope with emotions such as frustration and anxiety that might affect the way you make decisions or behave around other people.

This includes situations that might put you in a bad mood – a cold, wet football practice – and bigger disappointments – such as auditioning for a role and not getting the part or being beaten by a friend in a race.

Facing the **negative**

When you are working towards achieving a goal, it is very easy to get discouraged if things don't go to plan or you don't get the result you were hoping for. All sorts of things could happen: you can lose, be dropped, get injured or simply not improve at the rate you want. As a result, you might feel angry, sad, insecure, worried – a huge range of emotions that can affect your confidence. Believe me, I've been there.

I had my dream of winning a gold medal at the Olympic Games and I loved riding flat out on the track. But that didn't mean I found every day a doddle, just because I loved cycling – far from it! Most days, when I got out of bed, my legs were aching from all the hard training the day before. Sometimes I would train for weeks and not see any improvement in my times. There were races where I didn't do as well as I had hoped. And there were situations when I crashed and hurt myself so badly I wondered why I kept on racing at all!

Difficult moments

At different points on the journey towards my dream, I've experienced every single one of these emotions:

GRUMPINESS (JUST ASK MY PARENTS!) **ANGER** **SADNESS**

DISAPPOINTMENT **FRUSTRATION**

That's a lot of different emotions to learn to handle, often in situations where I'd worked extremely hard and the outcome really mattered to me. Sometimes, I've been pleased with the way I've handled things, and other times my emotions have got the better of me.

I've been in difficult situations where I've wanted to believe that it was my opponent's fault that I hadn't achieved my goal, or that there was a technical fault with my bike or that it had been bad luck that I'd lost or crashed. I wanted to blame anyone but myself for the negative emotions I was experiencing.

I remember a BMX semi-final, when I was ten, where immediately after the last jump my foot slipped off the pedal and no matter how hard I tried, I just couldn't get it back on quickly enough. Two riders overtook me and I lost a place in the final. I was in tears afterwards. I talked about it with my dad on the drive home. He helped me realize that it hadn't just been down to bad luck. I had thought I was home and dry, allowed myself to be distracted and then my technique fell apart. If I took a step back and thought about the situation clearly, without letting myself be influenced by how upset I felt, I could see that I was responsible for what had happened.

One of the most challenging moments in my Olympic journey came twelve months before my gold-medal-winning ride at the Athens 2004 Olympics. I was beaten in the National Track Championships by two teammates and, as a result, I wasn't sure if I would be selected for the GB team. I started to wonder if my dream was over. Perhaps this was the best I could be.

I was in a situation where I needed to take a step back and think through what had happened without letting my emotions cloud my judgement. I realized that I'd become so worried about what everyone else was doing that I was getting distracted from my own performance. I promised myself to start afresh and approach the twelve months leading to the Olympics with a better attitude. I would focus on what I needed to do to be my best and not worry about anyone else.

Time and time again, I've learned that the only person who has the power to truly change how you feel about a situation is … **YOU!** If you can take responsibility for how you react to things, ultimately you will be far more successful at what you are trying to achieve – even if it doesn't feel like it at that moment in time.

You have the power!

It doesn't matter what your goal is. It could be in sport, playing an instrument, drawing, cooking, your maths test – anything! Whatever it is, if you want to improve, you need to put yourself in situations that are going to challenge how you feel.

Every single day, in every situation, you can choose how you want to react. It's up to you whether you are going to throw your football boots across the changing room in a rage, or shake the hands of the team that beat you and look for ways to improve your performance.

Of course, it is harder to react positively in some situations than others and you can't solve every problem by changing your attitude. But if you go into a new day or practice session with a negative attitude, you can be pretty sure you'll have a bad time – because you will meet every challenge not as your best self. You have the power inside you to turn a negative into a positive and transform the situation. It's your superpower.

THINK ABOUT HOW YOU WOULD REACT IN THESE SIX SITUATIONS. CAN YOU FIND THE POSITIVES?

Attitude to practice

There's no way round this, whatever anyone says. How are you going to behave when practising is the last thing you feel like doing? Are you going to focus and give the session your absolute all? Or are you going to mess around and not really try?

Attitude to other people's success

You are not always going to be the best in the room. Often you won't even come close to being the best in the room! Will this make you want to give up or improve?

Attitude to feedback

People will tell you what they think you did well – and what they think you did badly! How are you going to take that feedback?

Attitude to advice

You are going to meet people on your journey who have more experience than you and who will be able to help you improve. Are you going to look for that help, or think you know it all?

Attitude to making mistakes or losing

You are going to get things wrong – and yes, most likely fail – along the way. This is 100 per cent normal and to be expected. But, in the heat of the moment, how are you going to react?

Attitude to setbacks

Sometimes things happen that are out of your control, such as injury or illness. How will you handle challenges?

It's all about attitude

When faced with a challenging situation, what will your attitude be? In the end, it all comes down to how you decide to react.

FEEDBACK
"He's wrong about my style. I'm a natural!"

PRACTICE
"It's raining, Dad. Can I skip practice?"

MISTAKES
"I got that question wrong. That proves I'm rubbish!"

OTHER PEOPLE'S SUCCESSES
"He's better than me, there's no point trying!"

ATTITUDE AWFUL

SETBACKS
"I'm injured, that's the end of the road!"

ADVICE
"Asking for help is embarrassing!"

Attitude Awful focuses on negative feelings or situations and what *can't* be done. It isn't interested in improving or asking others to help boost personal development.

FEEDBACK

"That's a great idea. I'll try and do that next time!"

PRACTICE

"I'm going to give this rehearsal my all!"

MISTAKES

"I'm disappointed, but I can see that I made a mistake on the start line."

OTHER PEOPLE'S SUCCESSES

"Ooh, she's really good at tackling! What's she doing that I'm not?"

ATTITUDE AMAZING

SETBACKS

"What exercises can I do despite my injury?"

ADVICE

"Can you help me improve that technique?"

Attitude Amazing always finds the positives, is open to advice and constantly looks for ways to improve. Taking this approach doesn't mean you should put your head in the sand and tell yourself that everything is great all the time, when it might not be. But it will mean that you take on each new challenge in the best possible frame of mind.

Champion Me

How can you train your brain to adopt Attitude Amazing? If you can become your own champion – and by that, I mean become your own biggest supporter and not rely on others to push you on – it will be huge step towards Attitude Amazing. Being self-motivated doesn't mean you can't have a coach, parent or teacher encouraging you, but you shouldn't be dependent on those people to get the most out of yourself.

Consider how you react to the other people around you and how they make you feel. Do you compare yourself to other people in a negative way?

She's so brilliant at it! I'll never be that good!
Well, he's a natural. I can't do that!
They're just better than us!
That team's always beaten us. There's no way we'll win this week!

Try not to do this! If you compare yourself to other people, you are setting yourself up for disappointment. You are creating a situation where if you fail to prove to yourself that you are better than your opponent at that moment in time, you will feel very negative about your abilities – when you shouldn't!

Your only opponent in your journey towards your goal should be yourself! Don't put yourself under pressure to work at someone else's pace. Learn from what you do well and what you could do better. You are working towards your *personal* best. At the end of the day, improving is all about ME vs ME!

That doesn't mean you can't learn from others. Part of having a positive attitude is being able to watch other people who are better than you, and rather than feeling threatened or panicked by their abilities, instead calmly think: *How are they doing that so well? How could I do that, too?* Don't be afraid to talk to these people and ask their advice, because no one improves in isolation.

Make sure you've found out everything you possibly can about your goal. Read all about it – use books, magazines and the Internet to find out tips, techniques or ideas. And don't forget to look after your body. Whatever you've set out to achieve will almost certainly be helped by a good night's sleep, and ensuring you aren't hungry or thirsty. It's far harder to be positive if you are tired or peckish!

Practise positive

A big test of your positive attitude will be something that we all find hard at times: practice. It can be hard to motivate yourself when you could be doing something that's more fun – or less challenging. I bet these two experiences are familiar:

> *It's been a long day at school and you are tired and hungry. You start catching up on your favourite show and scrolling on your phone. You REALLY don't feel like revising for the maths test right now.*

> *Your alarm goes off and you can't believe it's time to get up. You open the curtains and it's dark, wet and cold outside. You REALLY don't feel like heading to training right now.*

How do you motivate yourself to pick up your maths book or go outside on a rainy Saturday morning? Remind yourself of these important facts:

It's not supposed to be easy or everyone would do it!

I don't feel like it right now, but once I get stuck into the session, I know I'll be glad I did and I'll feel good afterwards.

Other people will be practising. I won't let them get a head start on me!

I will feel more in control of my performance and less anxious if I know I've practised for it.

These are the moments that make the difference in the long run. I can't expect to achieve my dream if I stop as soon as it requires me to dig a bit deeper!

Amazing Lives
Dance practice

I recently read that Beyoncé practised the same singing and dancing routine for eight months in preparation for a two-hour live stage show. I wonder how many of her fans who cheered and sang along with her knew how many hours and hours of hard work had gone into her performance? I bet many assumed that she was just an amazing singer and dancer and therefore the moves were easy for someone with her talent. But the reality is, Beyoncé has become one of the biggest stars on the planet because she worked hard, and has kept working hard to stay at the top.

"I wanted to sell a million records, and I sold a million records. I wanted to go platinum; I went platinum. I've been working non-stop since I was fifteen. I don't even know how to chill out."

BEYONCÉ

Positive feedback

It can sometimes be hard to listen to difficult feedback or comments on your performance, especially when you've really pushed yourself and tried your best. Remember that feedback is rarely being given to make you feel bad about yourself, but instead, it's there to help you improve! You shouldn't feel like it defines you, because as a person you are far greater than a piece of specific feedback on a technique or piece of homework. Separate it: it isn't personal, but it is a comment on what you've done in a situation.
If you can make this distinction, feedback is nothing to worry about.

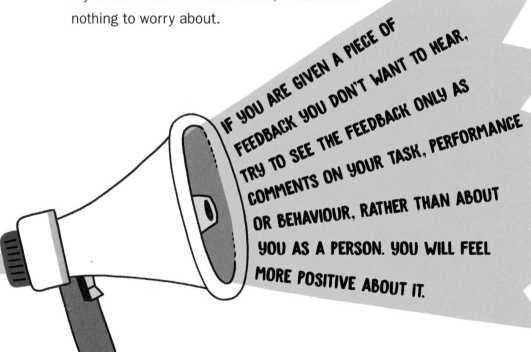

IF YOU ARE GIVEN A PIECE OF FEEDBACK YOU DON'T WANT TO HEAR, TRY TO SEE THE FEEDBACK ONLY AS COMMENTS ON YOUR TASK, PERFORMANCE OR BEHAVIOUR, RATHER THAN ABOUT YOU AS A PERSON. YOU WILL FEEL MORE POSITIVE ABOUT IT.

Positive people

It can also be hard to stay positive if you're surrounded by negativity. Look for people who give out positive energy – you will improve just by being around them. Try not to let other people drag you down; just understand that some people will not share your attitude. It's not your job to change them, but your positive approach might rub off on them – you never know!

LEAD FROM THE FRONT, BY BEING ENTHUSIASTIC, DETERMINED AND PASSIONATE ABOUT WHAT YOU DO. YOU'LL FIND THAT OTHER POSITIVE PEOPLE WILL WANT TO JOIN IN, TOO!

Choose smiling

The GB cycling team psychologist, Dr Steve Peters, used to tell us to smile on competition day. I remember thinking that it was strange! What difference could smiling possibly make to how fast I could pedal a bike around a track? The reason was simple! Smiling creates a positive outlook not only for yourself, but also for your teammates around you. Steve helped us build a positive environment, and that energy made the team stronger.

WHEN YOU HAVE A RACE, MATCH, AUDITION OR EXAM, REMEMBER TO SMILE! (AN ADDED BONUS IS THAT WHEN YOUR OPPONENTS SEE YOUR BIG GRIN, IT'LL SET THEM ON EDGE – THEY'LL BE WORRYING WHY YOU LOOK SO CONFIDENT!)

Staying positive in setbacks

As we've seen, it's easier to have a positive attitude when the going is good. What about when things get tough? Later on, we're going to look more closely at what happens when things within your control go wrong. But sometimes there are situations where there is nothing you can do other than stop what you're doing and take a moment to think how you can continue your journey in the most positive way.

Setbacks were a common experience in my cycling career, as they are for all sportspeople. I lost more races than I care to remember; I crashed; I was constantly trying to manage various injuries; I didn't always hit my training goals; I made loads of tactical errors in competitions; but the biggest setback I faced was having the event in which I was champion dropped from the Olympic programme in 2005.

Yes, you read that right! A year after winning a gold medal at the Athens 2004 Olympics, the 1,000-metre time trial was axed. This meant I wouldn't have the chance to defend my Olympic title. The event that I'd trained so hard for over the last twelve years was gone from the Olympics. I was devastated! At first, I refused to believe it. How could this be happening?! I was furious and I felt that it was unfair. But after a week or two, I realized that being angry, negative and moaning about it wasn't going to help me in three years' time at the Beijing 2008 Olympics. If I wanted to win another gold medal, I needed to change my attitude.

I had to totally reset my goals and I had to do it quickly, as time was running out and training for a new individual event would be a massive challenge. I hedged my bets and started training for two events: the sprint and the keirin, as I wasn't sure which one I would have the best chance in.

I used the vast knowledge and experience of my coaches to help speed up the learning process as much as possible. I focused on what I could do to improve; I watched video footage of the events over and over; I listened to every piece of advice I could get and I thought about how I could use my existing strengths as a rider to best effect in these different events.

In the end, thanks to the fantastic team of people around me, I made the transition into a sprint and keirin rider, and went on to win both events three years later in Beijing. And to top it off, we won the team sprint too! So there I was, with three gold medals in one Olympic Games, not a bad outcome from a setback that threatened to end my career! Sometimes adversity can force you to do things you didn't believe were possible.

THE NEXT TIME YOU FACE A SETBACK, STOP AND REFLECT. IS THERE SOMETHING POSITIVE YOU CAN LEARN FROM THIS? WRITE DOWN THE POSITIVE AND USE IT OVER THE COMING WEEKS AS YOU PLAN THE NEXT STEPS IN YOUR JOURNEY.

Injury time

If your goal is a physical challenge, it is also highly likely that you will experience an injury at some point. How do you use a positive attitude to your advantage in this frustrating situation?

 **DON'T**

Mope around, complaining and feeling sorry for yourself.

 DO

Focus on the things you are able to do, despite the injury.

When I severed the tendons in my right foot in an accident, my leg was in a plaster cast for eight weeks. Instead of sitting around feeling sorry for myself, I started a gym programme that focused on other parts of my body so I didn't lose fitness.

Staying positive during an injury is vital. Reset your plan, change your short-term stepping stones and keep smiling! It's vital you don't make your injury worse by exercising before it has healed, so follow the advice of your doctor or physio.

If your injury or illness requires you to have a complete rest, then think of ways to make progress other than from physical training. Watch videos of top performers in your sport to see if you can find areas to improve your technique. Visualize the perfect performance, so that when you start training again, you haven't forgotten what it feels like.

Sometimes injuries and illness are your body telling you it needs a rest not just physically, but mentally too. Have a break!

Overcoming setbacks

Jessica Ennis-Hill, a Great Britain heptathlete, was training hard for the Beijing 2008 Olympics. Based on her results leading up to the Games, she had a great chance of winning a medal, but disaster struck when she was forced to miss the championships with a stress fracture in her foot. Instead of feeling sorry for herself, she used the disappointment to fuel the fire in her belly. She set about getting over her injury and preparing for the next Olympics, which would be taking place in London in front of a home crowd. That was the motivation she needed.

Ennis-Hill famously went on to win the gold medal and become one of the biggest stars of the entire Games. Her victory was made all the sweeter by the fact that she had overcome the low points and bounced back with such determination.

If you can use setbacks to motivate you, like Ennis-Hill, you will increase the chance of achieving your dream.

"I'm proud of the way I've dealt with setbacks... You think, Why is the world doing this to me? But you have to pick yourself up again. That's what makes you a better athlete."

JESSICA ENNIS-HILL

Champion support

No matter how positive you are or how much potential you have, you can't achieve your dreams alone. Everyone needs support along the way.

Your family and friends are likely to be your biggest champions. They provide the love and security that give you the confidence to go out there and dream big, knowing that whatever happens, they'll be cheering you on. We all need encouragement like this, not just to reach our potential, but to be happy in life.

Never underestimate how important this is. A good way of showing the people around you how much you appreciate them is to be positive. If they see that you are enjoying chasing your dream, and that you're grateful for their encouragement, they'll be more likely to do everything they can to support you in the future. And don't forget it works both ways; make sure you are there to help them, too, when they need it!

TELL YOUR PARENTS OR FRIENDS NOW HOW MUCH YOU APPRECIATE THEM! SHOW YOUR POSITIVITY AND THANKS FOR THEIR EMOTIONAL SUPPORT AND BELIEF IN YOU.

Keep it going!

OK, so you now know why it's important to have a positive attitude.

You know that no matter where you start from, you are the person to get yourself on the right path to where you want to go.

You know that you can choose how you react to any challenge.

You know that by viewing a situation from a positive perspective it can help solve all kinds of problems, or get you through difficult times.

You know you have to take responsibility for your own actions, not make excuses, and be respectful of other people.

With all this information, you can use your new attitude to your advantage in all areas of your life.

But don't forget: the key to making the most of a positive attitude is consistency; in other words, you've got to keep doing it, through good days and bad!

Chapter *4*

GO FOR IT

PLANNING AND PRACTISING MAKE AMAZING

It's time to shine

**You know all about the power of being positive and you also know that there are going to be challenging situations along the way and you are ready to face them with a smile.
Now it's time for the hard work.**

How can you use the time you have to get the most amazing results? If you are willing to practise hard and make a plan, you will see progress in achieving your goals. So grab a pen and paper and let's go!

Talent vs hard work

How often have you seen someone on TV, YouTube or read about them online and thought:

Wow, what a talent!

She's a natural!

He was born to do that!

It's easy to watch a professional performing at the top of their game and just think that they've always been good at what they do because their talent just comes naturally to them.

If you see Serena Williams hitting a 100-miles-per-hour serve, Danny MacAskill doing a backflip over a huge jump on his bike, Ariana Grande performing onstage, you could be forgiven for thinking that because they make these feats *look* easy, that they *find* them easy.

The word "talent" is misleading. It can give the impression that a skill was learned without effort. The truth is that those professionals have only become the amazing tennis players, stunt cyclists and musicians they are today through years and years of planning, practice and preparation. They haven't been gifted their talent. They've all worked extraordinarily hard to unlock their full potential.

They might have certain advantages, such as their height or build, but those attributes didn't mean that they were born to be brilliant and that their success happened automatically. Instead, they've practised for thousands of hours towards their goal and they've shown determination and courage when things haven't gone to plan. You might have heard the saying: "It takes ten years to become an overnight success!"

Basically, there's no such thing as getting really good at something, really fast!

Plan one step at a time

Making a plan may sound a bit dull, but it will help you make the most of the months ahead of you by giving you a purpose.

You don't have to plan years in advance, but even thinking about the goals you would like to achieve in the weeks ahead will help you keep improving. When you set yourself a long-term goal (winning a gold medal, playing for a football team, performing at Glastonbury), it isn't in your control at that moment in time to achieve it. By thinking about the process (how to progress in the short-term), not the outcome (what the long-term result might be), you will stay motivated.

I once watched a documentary about a tightrope walker. He was going to walk across a huge, deep canyon without a harness or safety net! The interviewer asked him the question I was thinking: was he not scared of falling to his death?

He replied, "I don't even consider that outcome. I just focus on the process of putting one foot in front of the other. That's all I need to do. I keep repeating that and eventually the other side of the canyon comes to me."

Now I'm not suggesting you attempt anything like that! But it shows how focusing on one step at a time can stop you feeling daunted by how far away your end goal is – or how scary it is. Planning a series of stepping stones will help you work towards your big dream.

Smart steps

Any stepping stone in your plan should be carefully thought through so it has the maximum impact on your improvement. You need to think SMART:

* ✳ SPECIFIC *Have a clear aim.*
* ✳ MEASURABLE *Have a way you can measure your progress.*
* ✳ ACHIEVABLE *Make sure it is possible for you to achieve.*
* ✳ REALISTIC *Make sure it is possible to fit into your life.*
* ✳ TIMELY *Have a deadline.*

As I said in Chapter 2, my first stepping stone on my Olympic journey was to win the junior East of Scotland Championship. To hit that stepping stone, I created this SMART goal:

* ✳ SPECIFIC *Win the gold medal.*
* ✳ MEASURABLE *Practise on the hill where the race is taking place. Time each attempt to check progress.*
* ✳ ACHIEVABLE *I have finished fifth before, only a few seconds off the winning time. I can get close to the gold medal.*
* ✳ REALISTIC *My training needs to fit around my schoolwork.*
* ✳ TIMELY *I know exactly when I have to be race ready: on competition day!*

WRITE DOWN YOUR FIRST STEPPING STONE. DON'T THINK TOO FAR AHEAD — NEXT WEEK OR MONTH IS FINE TO BEGIN WITH!

Now you know how to create stepping stones, you can begin to build them up, so that each one is taking you closer to your big dream. To do this, you need to create a plan. Your plan doesn't need to be a grand, official document – you can just scribble it in a notebook. The key thing is that you don't keep it in your head, but you write it down.

The importance of writing things down applies to everything – it could be as simple as writing a revision timetable or as technical as a training programme for the Olympics. The action of writing down your goals on a piece of paper stores them securely in your long-term memory and therefore means you are more likely to succeed in them. In fact, scientific studies have shown that writing something down increases your chances of achieving it by up to 1.4 times! Amazing, huh?!

The best plan

DREAM: Get a good mark in my spelling test
PLAN

STEPPING STONE 1:
Make a list of my spelling words. Divide them into smaller sections to focus on.

STEPPING STONE 2:
Practise a different section every evening by writing the words out and saying them aloud.

STEPPING STONE 3:
Ask my mum to test me on each section at the end of each session.

DREAM: Improve the speed of my cricket bowling
PLAN

STEPPING STONE 1:
Decide with my coach on the optimal length run-up and practise it at training.

STEPPING STONE 2:
Build my body strength to improve overall fitness.

STEPPING STONE 3:
Once a week, have a practice session that is just focused on my technique.

WRITE DOWN YOUR PLAN FOR YOUR FIRST THREE STEPPING STONES. CONSIDER THE DECISIONS, ACTIONS, EFFORT, SUPPORT AND RESOURCES THAT YOU'LL NEED TO ACHIEVE EACH ONE.

The singer with a grand plan

Ed Sheeran has sold over 150 million records worldwide. He's also always had a plan for his music career. When his first album hit No. 1, he outlined in an interview the next steps his journey would take and the albums he was going to release.

The interviewer didn't believe him and thought he was being too ambitious! Seven years later, everything that Sheeran said he wanted to achieve had come to pass. And was Sheeran surprised by his success? No, he had been confident in his dream from the beginning, saying that as long as he was played on the radio, he knew his music would be loved by listeners.

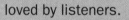

"Because the music I write is like love songs with big hooks, I kind of knew it would end up where it's ended up if it got the right radio play."
ED SHEERAN

Preparation

An important part of your plan succeeding is simply being organized. Think ahead to ensure you get the most out of your practice time. Ask yourself these questions:

1. What kit will you need? Is the weather forecast looking especially hot/cold/wet? How does that impact on the kit you need to bring? Is it clean and packed?

2. Is your equipment in good order and ready to go? If you do an activity that has special equipment (such as a bike or musical instrument), is it well maintained and prepped? Have you got the right books or your music?

3. Will you need food/drinks to give you energy and keep you hydrated before/during/after practice? If so, do you have some put aside and ready to take with you?

4. How are you getting to/from practice? Are you taking the bus? Are you getting a lift? Make sure you can get there on time.

5. What exactly are you planning to do in the practice session? What do *you* want to get out of it? It could be as simple as "I'm going there to have fun" – it doesn't need to be a super serious aim.

Putting in the hours

No matter what anyone says, practice is essential. If you want to improve, there are no shortcuts around the hours you need to put in. Contestants on a talent show who "suddenly" discover they have the voice of a superstar will most likely have been practising for many years before that moment. If I worked out how many hours I spent practising for my first gold medal, I think it would average out like this:

5 hours training a day, for 300 days a year, over a 12 year period
= 18,000 hours of practice

Practice is a continuous process – there are always more ways to improve! I'm not suggesting staying up all night before an exam or trying to get a personal best the day before a big race, but never think you know it all and therefore don't need to practise. Look for a new area to improve or find a different way of practising if you feel you have mastered what you are currently doing.

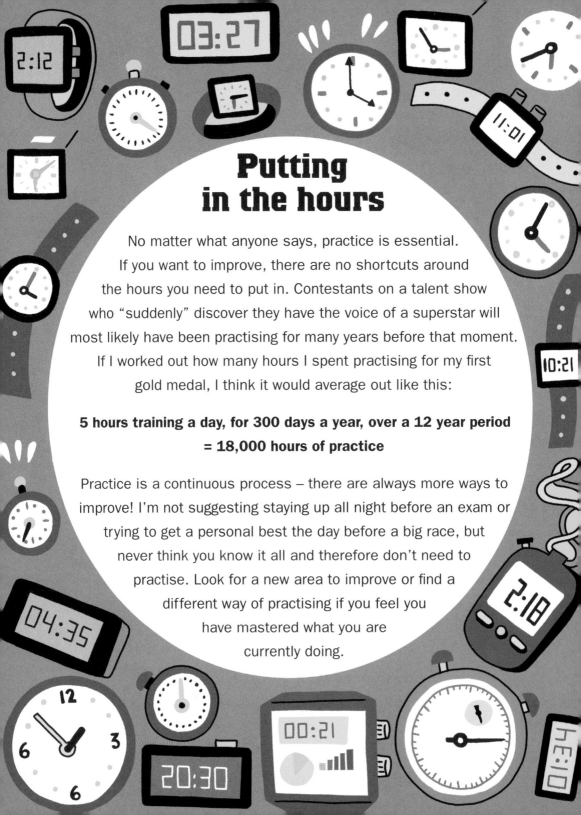

Practice time

Ellie Simmonds, the Paralympic swimmer, is no stranger to the punishing demands of a training schedule, both on the body and mind. Her training schedule involves her getting up at 4.30 a.m. and being in bed by 9.30 p.m. and, as well as swimming, it takes into account what she eats, and when she sleeps, rests and recovers.

In the run-up to the Paralympics, she trains nine times a week in the water, excluding gym work and yoga. A typical day sees her swimming first thing in the morning, then going to a gym session, before she has a nap and lunch. Then she is back in the pool swimming in the afternoon. But the hours of training have paid off: so far she has won eight medals at the Paralympics, five of them gold.

"Your friends and family know you're a professional swimmer, but they don't always understand the demands... All of it is time-consuming."
ELLIE SIMMONDS

Practise positively

Just doing the same old thing over and over again is unlikely to help you in the long term. You already know the power a positive attitude can have, but here are six tips that will help you get the most out of any practice session.

Prepare! You won't achieve your best in a practice session if you are tired, hungry or thirsty.

Focus! Don't practise aimlessly. Have an intention for what you want to work on or achieve within that session. You could even share your goal with your team, coach or teacher at the start of the session to really motivate you.

Push yourself! Practice should be challenging and intense. If you're finding it easy, you're not improving.

Keep it varied! Don't get stuck in a rut. Get your brain engaged by mixing up what you do.

Ask for help! People almost always want to help you and you can learn from their experience.

Keep at it! Little and often is far more effective than leaving a big gap and then cramming in the hours.

Unfortunately, there are only so many hours in a day, so you'll have to fit your practice around all the other things you have to do that can't be avoided, like going to school and doing your homework! Think about the spare time you have in your week and how much of that time you can use to practise. Write down as part of your stepping-stone plan:

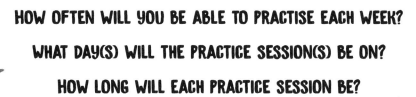

HOW OFTEN WILL YOU BE ABLE TO PRACTISE EACH WEEK?
WHAT DAY(S) WILL THE PRACTICE SESSION(S) BE ON?
HOW LONG WILL EACH PRACTICE SESSION BE?

Once you have a plan of how your practice will fit into your week, have a think about what you might want to do in each of the sessions to help you hit your SMART goals. It doesn't need to have a lot of detail, just write down a couple of words that will help you start each time with a clear focus of what you are going to do and how you are going to do it.

Improvement times

Remember that we all learn and improve at different rates:

- Some pick up new skills quickly, but then level off.

- Some take a long time to get the knack of what they are doing, but stick with it until eventually it clicks.

- Some make constant slow and steady progress, over many months or years.

What often happens when you take up something new is that you make big improvements at the beginning, because there is a lot to learn. As you get better, there are fewer obvious areas where you can improve, and eventually you stop making progress and level off. This is known as plateauing. It happens to all of us, so don't be surprised when it happens to you!

When you plateau, the natural reaction is to become frustrated. But don't keep looking backwards at what you've previously done, look forwards and think of new ways to improve. Try tweaking your routine and bring some fun elements back into your practice sessions. This helps to generate positive feelings, and don't forget: when you have fun, you will work harder!

We're all different!

We all grow and develop differently, too. This can have a huge impact on sporting performance, where being taller or physically stronger than your competitors is often a clear advantage.

When I was in my teens, I didn't have a big growth spurt until quite late on. I was playing rugby and I suddenly found myself at a disadvantage in terms of power and strength. I was taking big hits from heavier lads and I couldn't break through tackles. I went from scoring tries quite regularly to barely scoring at all! It was frustrating at the time, but it forced me to think around my disadvantage. If I wanted to keep up, I had to improve my technique. Becoming better at side-stepping meant that I was getting tackled less frequently. I also worked hard to get my positioning right when tackling other players so I could bring bigger opponents down to the ground without hurting myself.

As well as forcing me to improve my technique rather than just relying on brute force, my size disadvantage also toughened me up! When I finally had my growth spurt and caught up with the rest of the team, I was a much better player all round.

There will be periods when you feel like you aren't progressing towards your dream at the rate you want. At these times, it's important to remind yourself why you're doing what you do and, despite your frustrations, create a positive from the situation.

Building up your goals

Once you are confident with your stepping stones, set yourself a target to aim for the next month. It doesn't need to be huge, because a month isn't a lot of time to see big improvements, but it should be something that challenges you. It's a little step, but a step in the right direction. It helps to break down your long-term goal into smaller, more manageable targets that will eventually lead you there, if you keep hitting them.

Imagine you're climbing a MASSIVE mountain. You have just started your climb. If you keep looking at the very top, all covered in snow and clouds, it could become disheartening. Try not to think about how far away the top is and how long it'll take you to reach it. Instead, just focus on one step at a time. Every single step is taking you closer to the end goal at the summit of the mountain – and you should feel proud and positive about that.

WRITE DOWN YOUR STEPPING STONE FOR THE NEXT MONTH.

DON'T THINK:
I'm going to fail my maths test at the end of the month.

DO THINK:
I find long division hard. I'm going to focus on that this week.

DON'T THINK:
I'm going to be rubbish in the end-of-year concert!

DO THINK:
I'm going to ask my music teacher for another way of hitting that note.

DON'T THINK:
She's going to be picked for the hockey final, not me!

DO THINK:
She's really good at tackling. I'm going to watch her so I can try and copy the way she controls the ball.

Track your progress

As time goes by, remember that your plan is only for you. Don't feel that you have to show it to anyone else. Or, if you want to, share it with as many people as you like. Ask for their advice or guidance on how to make your plan even better.

Your plan shouldn't be used as a way to compare yourself to what other people are doing or have already done. Don't benchmark yourself against others' achievements; your ultimate aim is to be the best you can be, to get the most out of what you are doing and to have fun at the same time! Do that and the end result will take care of itself.

Your plan will start out as something you use a day or week at a time, but eventually, as you get used to your stepping stones and practice routine, you could move from scraps of paper to a notebook, diary or tablet so you have a permanent record of your journey.

It's easy to forget how far you've come, until you stop and look back at where you started. Writing a plan and then keeping a diary of what you do is a great way to see your progress over time. It's also useful to see if things aren't going quite as well as you'd hoped and gives you a chance to tweak what you're doing to help get you back on track. It needn't involve huge amounts of writing or take too much time. All you need to do is jot down in a few words what you did each day so you can remember in weeks, months or years to come.

The sorts of things you might write down could be:

WHAT TYPE OF PRACTICE YOU DID.
WAS IT REVISION, LEARNING YOUR LINES,
FITNESS WORK, TACTICS OR A COMPETITION?

WHAT WAS THE LENGTH OF TIME / DISTANCE /
LEVEL OF EFFORT? WERE THERE ANY MARKERS
OF HOW YOU PERFORMED?

HOW WOULD YOU RATE THE PRACTICE, 1–10? WHAT
DID YOU DO WELL? WHAT COULD YOU IMPROVE?

HOW ARE YOU FEELING, 1–10?

Amazing opportunities

Sometimes it's not just enough to want your dream and to have a plan for getting there. Dreams can cost money: from buying equipment, to travelling to competitions, coaching, entry fees, accommodation – even extra food for the energy you're burning!

So what do you do if you haven't got sufficient financial support? This isn't an easy one to solve. Depending on your activity, there are sometimes scholarships, funds or grants available. I was very lucky to receive funding from the National Lottery Sports Fund at a critical moment in my career. Another option is to get sponsored. It isn't easy, but if you can show potential sponsors how positive and hard-working you are, then you'll give yourself a much better chance of gaining support.

When I was competing in BMX races, it got to the point where we couldn't afford to keep travelling from Edinburgh to competitions all over the country every weekend. I needed to raise some money if I wanted to keep doing what I loved. We made a list of companies I could ask for sponsorship. We didn't have email, so it meant writing lots of letters, all by hand, explaining in detail exactly what I was aiming for and why I needed the company's support. I had to fit it in around my homework and training, so I would write a few letters every night before bed. This process took a couple of weeks, and as time went on, my positivity started to falter a little. I only received a few replies politely saying that they were unable to help me at this time. Then, finally, a letter arrived with good news! It was from Sir Tom Farmer, the CEO of Kwik Fit, a car tyre company based in Edinburgh. He invited me and my dad to his office for a chat. The day arrived and I suddenly got really nervous – I mean, this guy was on TV adverts!

Sir Tom was very friendly. He asked me to tell him about BMX and why I was looking for sponsorship. My dad started to answer, but Sir Tom asked that I told him in my own words. I talked about racing, why I loved it, my dreams and why we needed sponsorship to make that happen.

Once I finished, Sir Tom thanked us both and said he was really pleased to see that I was working hard towards a goal. He said Kwik Fit would be delighted to sponsor me £1,000 for the year, to go towards expenses. I was absolutely gobsmacked! We could now travel to races all over the country for the whole season. The money was a lifeline. It wasn't spent on a fancy new bike or kit; it paid for petrol, bed and breakfasts, and race entry fees. At the World Championships that year, I proudly raced with Kwik Fit logos on my helmet and jersey.

Recognize opportunities and grab them when they come along – even if they weren't part of your original plan. If you have the chance to meet someone exciting and tell them about your dream, then go for it!

It's OK to change your plan!

You may find there are times when you feel like you aren't enjoying chasing your dream as much as you used to. That's OK! Don't feel pressure to continue something when you really don't enjoy it, but at the same time don't give up just because of a short-term performance dip. Such dips are totally normal.

Rather than struggling with something you aren't enjoying, or dropping it during a dip and regretting it later on, there is another option: changing direction and trying something else.

When I was about thirteen, I stopped enjoying BMX racing. I still loved riding my bike, but I felt like I needed a different challenge. Mountain biking was taking off as a new sport and I decided to try it. I absolutely loved it! It was close enough to BMX that I didn't have to start from scratch; I had the bike-handling skills and the leg power, but there were loads of new and exciting things to learn.

I went down a different route than I had planned, but, without realizing it at the time, it was a step closer to me discovering another type of cycling a few years later, which would end up being my all-time favourite – track cycling on the velodrome!

Now get cracking!

Right, you've written down a rough plan. It might only be a few words on the corner of a piece of scrap paper, but it is a start! It should give you the feeling that you have a map to lead you to where you want to be. Plan further and further ahead in order to aim for your longer-term goals. These, in turn, will act as bigger and bigger stepping stones towards your main goal.

**So, we're getting there!
You've been inspired, set yourself a goal and now you have a positive attitude and a plan of action. What's next? Go out there and make some champion mistakes!**

Chapter **5**
FANTASTIC FAILURE
WHY LOSING IS MORE AMAZING THAN YOU THINK

It's failure time

Nobody is perfect and everyone is going to fail
at some point. In fact, failure is a very important part
of achieving a dream, because it's where you learn
the most about yourself and what you are trying to do.
Rather than thinking of failure as something to fear,
I want you to see it as an important step
in your journey to amazing.

Nothing truly worth having comes easily and you'll soon
realize how much more satisfying it is to achieve things when
you've had to work hard for them. You are going to fail, make
mistakes, feel stupid, come last, get beaten or not be selected
along the way – that's guaranteed! The important thing is how
you react to these failures and use them to your advantage in
the future.

Right then – it's time to roll up your sleeves, get
stuck in, and make some mistakes.

And trust me on this – there will be some absolute stinkers along the way!

Nobody is perfect.

Every single person in the history of humankind has failed at something.

Every single person.

That means no one is perfect.

The greatest sportspeople, inventors, actors, scientists, musicians, artists and singers that the world has EVER seen have all had rejections, defeats and disappointments along the way. When you find out more about people who have become successful, you will discover that most of these champions have been inspired by their setbacks and used them to push themselves even harder.

THE GREAT LEGEND OF ROBERT THE BRUCE AND THE SPIDER

I want to tell you a story I heard many times as a kid growing up in Scotland.

ONCE UPON A TIME, a man named Robert the Bruce ruled as King of Scotland from 1306 until 1329. He fought tirelessly for Scotland's independence from England.

When Edward I, the King of England, invaded Scotland, Robert was driven into hiding and took refuge in a cave. His spirits were low and he felt close to giving up. How could he go on, having tried and failed so many times to defeat Edward and set Scotland free?

As he sat in the cold, damp cave, he spotted a spider trying to make a web, but without any success. It kept trying but it couldn't make the threads stick. Time and time again the spider would fall, but still get back up to keep trying. Finally, the spider began to weave its web.

Robert was so inspired by its unwillingness to give up, that he went back to his men and told them: "If at first you don't succeed, try, try and try again!" The Scots went on to defeat the English at the Battle of Bannockburn in 1314, and Scotland became an independent country.

I love this story, partly because my grandpa was the first person to tell it to me, but also because it shows the importance of persistence, even when you think the odds are against you.

Amazing Lives

The rower who refused to give up

Katherine Grainger, the Great Britain rower, knows the importance of persistence. In the Sydney 2000 Olympics, the Athens 2004 Olympics and the Beijing 2008 Olympics, she won silver medals in her rowing events. In every close-fought final over a twelve-year period, Katherine failed to achieve her dream of being an Olympic champion.

Was this simply the best she could be? Would she retire from the sport with her head held high, having won three Olympic silver medals? Nobody would ever have thought less of her if she had, but she was determined that gold was still a possibility. She vowed to come back stronger.

In the London 2012 Olympics, Katherine and her rowing partner dominated the final in front of an overjoyed home crowd, crossing the finish line with a comfortable lead to claim the gold medal. She had used the results of the previous three Olympic Games to drive her on to even greater things.

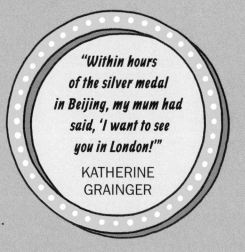

"Within hours of the silver medal in Beijing, my mum had said, 'I want to see you in London!'"

KATHERINE GRAINGER

FACING YOUR FEAR

Fear of failure often stops us pursuing our dreams. No one wants to try something and then look stupid if it doesn't go to plan. But if you are able to overcome a fear of failure, you will unlock a whole world of possibility.

Let me tell you the story of my good friend Jason Queally, one of my teammates from the GB cycling team. He was held back for many years by a fear of failure.

He had the physical potential to be successful in a number of different sports. But whenever the chance came along to take a risk and go beyond his comfort zone, he wouldn't take it. He said that the turning point in his sporting career was the moment he realized his own fear of failure was stopping him from discovering what he was capable of.

When he was twenty-five, he decided to try cycling. For the first time in his life, he really threw himself at the task in hand. He decided to ignore his negative thoughts about failure and fully committed to the new challenge, with no excuses and no backing out when it got tough.

His progress was incredible. Within eighteen months, he won a silver medal at the National Track Championships; within three years he won a Commonwealth Games silver medal and by the time five years had passed, the unthinkable happened: he won a gold medal at the Sydney 2000 Olympics! That gold medal was one of the biggest drivers of GB's cycling success over the following two decades.

His journey was remarkable, but like everyone's, not without setbacks, either. He was badly injured in a crash when a half-metre long piece of broken wood from the track surface stuck into his back. It took a major operation to remove it, and he was left with over seventy stitches and a huge scar as a reminder!

Like all great champions, he didn't give up. He used his injury to change direction slightly and focus on the 1,000-metre time trial for the Olympics in Sydney. He set about becoming the best in the world in this event – and he did!

The "old" Jason Queally wouldn't have put himself in the position to fail or get beaten. He would have stayed within his comfort zone as a big fish in a small pond. But his new attitude allowed him to truly realize his potential.

It's so much easier never to put yourself into a position where you might fail or look a bit silly, than to go for it and take a chance. But life would be boring if we stayed within our comfort zones and never took on challenges.

Is fear holding you back?

You might never lose the fear of failing entirely. But there are ways in which you can make sure it isn't holding you back.

First of all, stop thinking that everything depends on the outcome. Instead, be proud of the hard work you are putting in and acknowledge all the small achievements and positives you are experiencing along the way. It's not all about the end result!

Those who fear failure are more likely to think the outcome defines them as a person. They believe that if they don't win a medal, their entire life is a failure! Of course you should care about your dream, but it is important to remember that your success or failure in that activity is just a small part of the amazing person you already are. Your life does not depend on winning a race, scoring a goal or getting a part!

It's easy to be too hard on yourself, and it's sometimes difficult to see things from the right point of view when you are so close to it all. When you step back and look at the bigger picture, it can really help to get things in perspective.

IN YOUR DIARY, KEEP A LIST OF ALL THE EXPERIENCES THAT MAKE YOU FEEL HAPPY, POSITIVE AND PROUD OF YOURSELF. THE NEXT TIME YOU FEEL WORRIED ABOUT FAILING, TAKE FIVE MINUTES TO LOOK BACK AT THE LIST OF THE AMAZING THINGS YOU'VE ALREADY ACHIEVED.

How to handle failure

OK, so we now know that failure is something to expect. It's not a matter of if it will happen, but *when*. But with all that said, there are still certain phrases that none of us really enjoy hearing, especially when we've worked hard and given something our all:

How do you stop yourself losing confidence when you encounter failure or disappointment? The feeling of your stomach dropping at an unexpected result is never nice. How can you approach the situation positively and use the experience to your advantage?

The first thing to do is to take responsibility for your actions and own your performance. That's basically just a grand way of saying, "Don't make excuses!" When it goes wrong, don't look for other people or situations to blame, just accept that it didn't work this time. Then go away and work out how to do it better next time.

FOUR DIFFICULT BUT IMPORTANT QUESTIONS

When you are in a situation that hasn't turned out quite how you expected and you feel that you have in some way failed, ask yourself these four questions.

1. DID YOU DO YOUR BEST?

Be honest with yourself. Did you try your hardest? If so, then well done! That's all any of us can do. Keep measuring your progress against your own previous personal bests. If you are seeing even the slightest improvement, then you are doing a great job! If you feel that you didn't try your hardest, well, that's what you need to try to change next time around. Go back to your goals and find your focus and intensity.

2. DID YOU LOSE TO A STRONGER OPPONENT?

Until you reach your end goal, there will almost always be someone out there who is "better" than you at your chosen activity. They might be more experienced or they might be bigger or stronger than you.

Don't let that get you down: it's just the way life is! Never compare yourself to others. Only compete with yourself. Use others to learn from, or to inspire you, but don't become demoralized at how much better they are than you at the moment. They were beginners once, too!

3. IS THERE A REASON WHY YOU ARE NOT MAKING THE IMPROVEMENT YOU EXPECTED?

You feel that you've hit a sticking point and aren't getting better; perhaps you even feel like you're going backwards. Don't worry; this is to be expected at times! Is there anything that you could do differently – across your technique, training or attitude – which might give you better results? Think about someone you could ask for advice, such as your coach or teacher.

4. ARE YOU GETTING TOO WORRIED ABOUT THE END GOAL?

If you become too focused on your end goal, you will put pressure on yourself and are more likely to underperform. This can happen to absolutely anyone – even the best in the world – if they don't control how they view their situation. So remember to focus on your stepping stones. Don't get swept away by thinking too far ahead, but have fun doing what you do!

These questions aren't always easy ones to answer, but if you can be honest with yourself you will have a far better chance of learning from the experience.

How to turn failure into a POSITIVE

Making mistakes is an important part of improving, so use the experience to inspire you to be better prepared for your next challenge – both physically and mentally. After you experience a failure it's important to take time to think about what you learned about yourself, your behaviour and others.

Did you respond to the situation in the best possible way?

Look at the preparation you did before the match, event or exam. Did you prepare as well as you could? What could you have done differently to avoid making the mistake?

Were you relying on a lucky charm or ritual? It's easy to have a lucky pair of socks or pants, or a special necklace. But then what happens if you forget to bring them on an important day? You need to believe that anything you achieve is because of your hard work, not because of luck. Of course, we often experience good and bad luck, but we don't have any control over it, so free yourself from that worry!

How did you respond in the moment when things went wrong? Did you recover your performance, or did you let the mistake get to you and, as a result, lose your concentration and focus for the rest of the time?

Did you let another person or opponent affect your performance? Were you able to move on or did it change the way you performed?

Think about how you behaved and how you felt and what you would do next time you are in that situation. Remember that ultimately the person most in control of improving your performance is ... YOU!

How to be an amazing
LOSER!

When you're competing in sport, the main aim is to win, right? Well, I'd argue that's only half right.

Let me explain. Of course you always want to win, and you should try your best to win in any competition, but sometimes winning is very unlikely due to the high standard of the event.

You might be competing against someone older or bigger who has an advantage in strength or weight. They might also be more experienced than you. If you get beaten by an opponent, don't despair – try and learn from the other's strengths. There will be some important positives to take away.

You might have produced a personal best, but still lost. If that's the case, then you should be patting yourself on the back! You can only do your best, remember!

You might have made a big mistake, or a tactical error that lost the match for your team, or the race for yourself. You might not have done enough training or preparation. But if you can identify what went wrong and know how to avoid doing it again, then it was well worth making that mistake!

And you may have gone into the event with high expectations and been thoroughly defeated by better opponents: in that situation, there's only one thing you must do.

BLAME THE REFEREE?

CALL THE OTHER TEAM CHEATS?

COME UP WITH AN EXCUSE?

NO!

You shake the hand of your opponent(s) and congratulate them.

WELL DONE!

They were better than you on the day and sometimes you have to accept that! But … it doesn't mean they'll always be better than you.

Just make a promise to yourself, there and then, that you'll come back next time even better prepared and that they'd better be too, if they think they're going to beat you again!

The gracious loser

If you ever see tennis legend Roger Federer interviewed after a Grand Slam final, he is always positive, regardless of whether he's won or lost. If he wins, he never takes full credit, but thanks his support team and family, then talks about what a great battle it was against his opponent. If he loses, he congratulates the winner, makes no excuses, but pledges to come back stronger next time.

It's no surprise that he has such a huge fan base, all around the world. He has respect for his opponents and for the sport itself. The next time you have a big disappointment and are having a hard time dealing with it, remember Roger and think, *What would he do in this situation?* If someone who's won more Grand Slam tennis titles than any male player in history can be positive in defeat, then you can, too!

"Sometimes you have to accept that a guy played better on the day than you."
ROGER FEDERER

Not being selected

I remember waiting for the rugby team list to go up on the noticeboard every Friday, and the nervousness I felt checking it to see if my name was there. It was always a buzz to make the team, but there were times when I didn't, and that really hurt.

Looking back now, rather than being grumpy or sulking, it would have been better to try and find the positives in the situation:

"I'm playing in a lower team, so that means I should have a better chance of showing my skills to the coaches, playing a blinder, scoring a few tries and reminding them that I should be back in the first team next week!"

"As a reserve, sitting on the bench, I'll show great team spirit, cheer the lads on, and when the time comes be ready to sprint onto the pitch with fresh legs and do my best for the team!"

We don't always behave the way we should, or the way we really want to; it takes experience to learn how to be positive when things aren't going our way.

It's also important to look out for your teammates when they go through the unpleasant experience of getting dropped. When you get selected, somebody has to make way for you, so don't forget to speak to them when that happens, and make sure they're doing OK. Encourage them to stay positive too. That's what being in a team is all about – looking out for each other!

You're amazing, but never invincible!

No matter how good you are, never believe that you are unbeatable. If you do, all it takes is one defeat (which will happen), and it will burst your bubble of confidence. Sure, losing hurts, but defeats can be motivating. Winning also doesn't necessarily mean that you will keep improving.

I became world champion for the first time in 2002. Stepping onto the podium to receive my gold medal was magical. On that day, at that moment, I was the fastest in the world! But it changed my outlook on the way I trained and prepared for the World Championships the next year. You see, I felt that I now had the winning formula for being the best. Why would I want to change it? I became fixated on doing exactly the same as I'd done the year before, hoping to repeat the same result.

The trouble was the standard of the race was getting higher. I had upped my game in the run-up to the 2002 championships and now my opponents were plotting to do the same.

I arrived at the 2003 World Championships, aiming to defend my title, but it didn't go to plan. I repeated the same performance from twelve months earlier, but this time around, that was only good enough for fourth place.

I was devastated. I had lost my world champion title, but more importantly, with a year to go until Athens, I felt that my dream of an Olympic gold medal was slipping through my fingertips…

So what did I do to turn it around? With my team, I sat down and took a long hard look at everything I had done that season. Looking ahead to the Athens 2004 Olympics, I wasn't afraid to make changes, because now I had nothing to lose!

I approached the year as a contender not a champion. I felt like I had the fire back in my belly. I arrived in Athens in the form of my life, and as you found out in Chapter 1, it went pretty well!

That whole experience taught me how crucial it is not to let yourself get too down when things go wrong. Instead use the frustration to make you work even harder. Always look for ways to tweak what you do so you keep improving. Failure is where all the lessons are; winning feels great, but you will learn so much more when it doesn't all go to plan.

So, go out there, try your hardest. Make mistakes, get beaten, come last, trip up, fall over, forget your lines, miss the penalty, drop the ball, score an own goal – but remember: it happens to everyone! Those low points will make the high points all the sweeter when they eventually come along.

Chapter 6
ENJOY IT!
HAVE FUN AND BELIEVE IN HOW AMAZING YOU ARE

There is one final thing you need to do to become your own champion. If you want to get the best out of yourself, you have to have fun! I know that I'm repeating myself when I say this, but it's so important for your journey to amazing.

The enjoyment you get from your chosen passion – whether it's swimming, cycling, singing or gaming – will be the single biggest thing that pushes you on and keeps you motivated. If you have fun, you will want to come back for more, time and time again.

So how do you keep enjoying yourself, day in and day out, through the good times and the bad? A big part of it is learning to take control of your emotions so you feel positive regardless of the situation. That takes confidence and self-belief – things that we all have to work on at times.

Believe in your AMAZING self

Have you ever waited on the start line of an event and felt like you didn't belong there? Or felt that everyone else in a group was better than you? Well, if you have, then you're not alone.

Let me tell you a secret. When I started racing at international level, I didn't enjoy it all that much! Whenever I lined up against a rider from another country, I found it pretty stressful. I felt that rider deserved to be there, whereas I wasn't sure that I did. I lacked both self-belief and self-confidence. Sure, I had my dream and I was working incredibly hard to achieve it, but if I'm honest, I didn't truly see myself as a potential future champion. I thought champions were a different breed to the rest of us ordinary people.

At that point, I didn't realize that we all have the capability to go far beyond what we think is possible.

What changed things was the incredible success of Jason Queally at the Sydney 2000 Olympic Games. Seeing the first British rider for decades win a gold medal in a sprint event was a turning point for me.

In Jason's success I saw what hard work and planning could achieve, particularly because I'd always seen Jason as a normal guy, like you or me. If he could become an Olympic champion, then maybe I could get close to becoming one, too...

See your SUCCESS

Having confidence in yourself is absolutely vital to being the best you can be – not just in sport or whatever your chosen passion is – but for life in general. I've become a big believer in the saying "If you can see it, you can achieve it!"

That means both visualizing every aspect of your dream (which we looked at in Chapter 2) and also looking out for other people who have had success in your chosen activity and using them to inspire you.

THINK OF AN AMAZING PERSON WHO IS SIMILAR TO YOU IN TERMS OF THEIR OUTLOOK, AGE OR PHYSICAL BUILD. PERHAPS THEY ARE IN YOUR CLASS, ON YOUR TEAM OR ONE OF YOUR OPPONENTS. IF THEY CAN DO IT, THERE'S NO REASON WHY YOU CAN'T, TOO!

Once I had seen Jason Queally's success, I started to gain confidence in myself. I began to feel that I *did* belong in the Great Britain team and that I *did* deserve to compete at international level. Suddenly, my enjoyment of racing increased. If my teammates and the people I was competing against could become champions, so could I! Unlocking my self-belief made competitions something to look forward to instead of dreading.

Believing in yourself doesn't mean that you automatically think you're the best, or that you have complete confidence in your ability to do really well all the time. It's about understanding you belong on that stage, pitch, track or in that classroom as much as anyone else, simply by the virtue of being the person that you are and the fact that you are passionate about what you do!

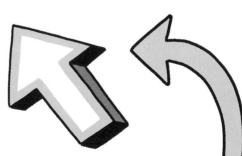

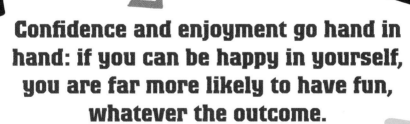

Confidence and enjoyment go hand in hand: if you can be happy in yourself, you are far more likely to have fun, whatever the outcome.

Face challenges with
confidence

Having self-confidence doesn't mean that your journey will be fun every second of the way. But if you can face challenges believing in yourself from the outset, you will be far more likely to overcome those obstacles.

As a kid at school, I used to hate having to talk in front of the whole class. I dreaded the thought of being singled out to answer a question. What's strange is that I was quite confident outside the classroom and would be happy to crack jokes with groups of friends, no problem at all. By the time I got to high school, I would do anything to avoid talking to a large group of people. It was the same at university too.

But the trouble with avoiding the things that you lack confidence in is that you never get better at them. When I left university, I thought I wouldn't have to worry about it ever again. But when I started to do well in cycling, it meant that I began to get invitations to speak at public events. That meant me talking on a stage to a crowd of strangers. *Aaarrrggh!!!*

I realized that if I wanted to achieve my full potential in cycling, then I would have to get used to speaking in public. So I forced myself to do it. It wasn't great at first. I was nervous walking up onstage, holding the microphone, hearing my voice through the speakers and seeing a group of faces staring at me. Gradually, I got used to it and began not to dread it quite so much.

After I gave talks or did events, people would come up and talk to me. But, guess what! Despite my fears, no one ever said:

> Chris, you absolutely fluffed up that introduction. What an idiot!

> Chris, you looked like a muppet up there onstage!

> Chris, you were really droning on. That was so boring!

Instead, they came up to ask me questions or share their own stories. Sometimes, they congratulated me for speaking well! Of course, it always helps to get positive feedback. But it also boosted my confidence that I didn't get any negative feedback, either. I had faced my biggest fear and none of the bad things I had expected to happen had actually happened!

I had got past the negative voice in my head. Public speaking just took time and practice like any other skill. My confidence grew to the point where I was happy to stand up in front of thousands of strangers and make a speech – and actually enjoy doing it. When I accepted an award at the BBC Sports Personality of the Year ceremony, there were 12,000 people in the audience! As it went silent I thought, *Wow, I can't believe I'm going to speak to so many people!* Once, I would never have thought that was possible.

How to handle pressure

Sometimes the desire to do well in a certain situation – such as a race or exam – can put you under pressure and the fun gets pushed aside.

When I was competing, whether as a kid in BMX or as an adult at the Olympic Games, people would often come up to me right before a race and say:

CHRIS, JUST GET OUT THERE AND ENJOY IT!

I would be thinking:

ENJOY IT? ENJOY IT?! YOU HAVE NO IDEA HOW MUCH PRESSURE I FEEL RIGHT NOW!!!

And yet, as soon as the race was over, every single time, no matter whether I won or not, I would always end up thinking:

THAT WASN'T SO BAD! ACTUALLY, THAT WAS REALLY FUN! I CAN'T WAIT FOR THE NEXT RACE!

Over time, I began to expect this feeling of pressure. I was stepping (well, pedalling!) out into the unknown. Despite all the planning, preparation and practice I'd done, I didn't know what was going to happen during the next few minutes and that was making me feel nervous.

The fact is, nerves and excitement make our bodies produce adrenaline, a chemical that gives you the feeling of butterflies in your stomach. Adrenaline increases blood flow to your muscles and makes you feel more alert. If you can learn to stay calm when you feel that tingle of adrenaline, it will help you perform at your very best. Don't dread the feeling: adrenaline is your friend!

NEXT TIME YOU FEEL NERVOUS OR UNDER PRESSURE, TAKE A DEEP BREATH AND REMIND YOURSELF OF ALL THE HARD WORK AND PREPARATION THAT YOU'VE PUT IN. TELL YOURSELF THAT YOU'RE READY FOR THE CHALLENGE. USE THE ADRENALINE!

You will experience anxiety and doubt on your journey, but remember that it is normal to feel that way and it doesn't mean you have fallen out of love with what you do. When you feel under pressure or aren't enjoying yourself, remind yourself of the happiness you felt when you first discovered your passion. If you're still struggling with those feelings, go back to basics. Don't worry about plans, targets, results, goals, dreams, just go out and do the thing you love for the sake of it. Do it for fun!

Fight the FOMO!

Another, almost certain, way to spoil your enjoyment is to worry that everyone else is doing something way cooler than what you've chosen. Beware of constantly wishing you were somewhere else, doing something different.

Fear of missing out, or FOMO, has become a recognized phenomenon. So many people post pictures and stories on social media that show them always living their best life. It's easy to fall into the trap of comparing your life to theirs and wishing yours was a bit more exciting.

But before you get FOMO, don't forget that photos and posts can often be misleading. Nobody bothers to post online the boring and everyday stuff that we all have to do. Imagine what those posts would look like!

Just tidying my bedroom!

Cleaning my football boots! #nofilter

Off to the dentist later on – can't wait!

The grass isn't greener on the other side; it just looks like it is. So don't worry about what others are doing. Chasing your dream won't be glamorous all the time, trust me! At the end of the day, you make your own enjoyment by getting to do what you love, so stay focused on your journey.

Keep the good times rolling

How do you keep enjoying what you do, day in, day out, through the good times and the more challenging ones? Well, the following tips can help:

- Do it for yourself. Not for your parents, your coach or anyone else. Live your own life. The more you try to please other people, the more pressure you'll feel and the harder it will be to enjoy yourself.

- Use your goals to motivate you, but don't let them get you down because they seem unachievable. They should inspire you, not be another source of pressure.

- Keep a fun element in every session you do. We would often muck around on the velodrome during our warm-down after each training session, practising skills and manoeuvres that were a laugh but not part of our main training programmes.

- Enjoy the small things: the jokes you have with your friends in the cast or group you practise with. Those things matter just as much as your goals and dreams.

And, of course, as you already know, DON'T FORGET TO SMILE!

Stay motivated

So what happens when you keep smashing your personal bests and hit the goals and stepping stones you've laid out to help you along the way?

CELEBRATE THEM — YOU'VE EARNED IT!

SAVOUR THOSE MOMENTS!

SOAK THEM UP!

But also remember the feelings of joy and happiness and commit them to memory. You will need them when you're struggling for motivation further down the road.

After big events, or significant steps forward, you might find yourself feeling a bit flat or lacking in motivation, as the buzz from that excitement wears off. This is known as an anticlimax and is completely normal, so don't worry.

This is often the best time to return to your plan, look back over what worked and what could have been better, so you know for next time. Then reset, have a small break to recover and start aiming for the next stepping stone.

This cycle will hopefully happen many times along your journey, as you hit your targets and move on to the next one, higher and higher each time.

Success doesn't always mean happiness

It's easy to confuse enjoyment with success, but they don't always mean the same thing. Some of the happiest people I've ever met haven't "won" anything and, on the other hand, some of the most successful people on the planet are miserable.

There is a type of person who achieves their goal of becoming an Olympic champion, but, despite succeeding at their dreams, they aren't happy or contented. Along the way, they've somehow stopped enjoying what they do and the gold medal at the end hasn't magically changed their lives for the better.

One of my teammates used to moan every day about how much they hated being a professional cyclist. They were counting down the days to the Olympics and their retirement! Rather than enjoying the journey, they just wanted to reach the end as quickly as possible. Their approach was a bit like fast-forwarding through a film to watch the final five minutes!

But there is another type of person. Some of my teammates weren't selected for the Olympics or didn't win a medal. But they had the right attitude, worked incredibly hard, learned a huge amount and, even though they didn't quite achieve their ultimate dream, they had a blast chasing it.

It's a piece of cake

What does this mean for you? Well, it's certainly not an excuse to give up on your dreams! You can get to the top and have fun along the way, I promise you.

But your gold medal, or whatever it is that you've set as your ultimate goal, should always be seen as the cherry on top of the icing on the cake. It's that little extra special something which makes an already great thing even more brilliant!

That cherry isn't everything. It's the finishing touch.

The delicious cake, the main part of what you do, is the joy that comes from having a passion and pursuing it. It's the people you meet and the experiences you have together along the way. It's the satisfaction of making progress towards your dream.

In fact, if you don't enjoy the day-to-day routine of what you do, the chances are you won't ever achieve your true potential, because it will become a chore and something you don't look forward to. That isn't a recipe for long-term success!

Some of the best moments of my life so far have been winning bike races and medals, and I feel incredibly fortunate to have those incredible memories to look back on. But if someone asked me what I enjoyed most about my cycling career, it definitely wouldn't only be the competitions and medal ceremonies that came to mind.

More often, my best memories are related to the random funny moments that happened in all sorts of places other than on the track itself: in airports, buses, gyms, restaurants, hotels, press conferences, meetings, parties and so on – often in countries that I would never have visited had it not been for cycling.

Sharing these moments with my teammates, friends and family, having the stories to retell every time you get back together, years later, is without doubt the best part of having had the opportunity to chase my dream.

What's important to YOU?

I want to end by leaving you something to think about.

Dr Steve Peters, the GB cycling team psychologist, once asked me a question, with the aim of helping me get some perspective on how important I thought it was to win bike races.

He asked me to imagine myself as an old man (yes, even older than I am now!) sitting down to talk to my grandkids.

He asked me what I would say to them, as my final piece of advice, on how to get the most out of their lives. In other words: what did I think was important in life?

Now, this was quite a deep question, but one that I didn't have to think too long or hard about. Really it seemed pretty straightforward. I imagined telling my grandkids to be kind, to treat other people the way they would hope to be treated themselves, to be happy and to give their best in whatever they choose to do.

I certainly didn't imagine myself telling them that it was important to be the fastest in the world at riding bikes round and round in circles!

This doesn't mean your goals aren't important or worth chasing. They are, and more than anything, I want you to go out there and become your own greatest and best champion in whatever you dream of doing. It just means it can be helpful to remind yourself sometimes that those goals and dreams aren't everything and they don't define you.

If you can keep that in mind when you're going through a difficult patch, hopefully that might help bring you back to why you chose your passion to begin with.

Because it is fun and you love it!

In the end, it really is that simple.

So that's a bit about my journey.

I've shared some of the things I've learned and what I've discovered to be important. I hope it will help you to start a journey of your own. Who knows where it could lead?!

I also wanted to tell you how much I've enjoyed writing this book. Thank you for giving me a reason to sit down and put all these ideas and thoughts onto paper. Like anything worth doing, it wasn't easy, but it has given me a huge sense of satisfaction bringing it to life and seeing it through to the end. Oh, and in case you're wondering – being an author is another thing that I never imagined I could do!

If you can take away just one thing from this whole book and keep it in mind as you go through life, it's that you have the potential to do way more than you could ever believe is possible. Trust me. Every single one of us does. If I can become a champion, so can you.

As you know, this doesn't mean your dream will land in your lap, or that it's going to be easy. It won't. But if you can use the ideas I've talked about and apply them to your situation, I promise you that you'll be amazed at what you can achieve.

Life is full of so many wonderful opportunities and experiences and you need to grab them with both hands. YOU make it happen! Don't worry about what everyone else is doing; this is your journey to find your personal best. Believe in yourself, have the confidence to take on new challenges without the fear of failing. And when you make mistakes, learn from them.

I would love to hear from you! Please do get in touch to let me know what you thought of the book, and how you're getting on chasing your dream.

So, good luck! I really hope you find your inspiration, then aim high, make a plan, stick with it and stay positive – even when you don't succeed first time round. But the most important thing of all is, of course, to enjoy it!

Right, that's enough from me. Now it's over to you. I'm excited, and I hope you are, too!

Get out there and be amazing!

With thanks to...

This has been a hugely enjoyable book to write.
It has allowed me to reflect on some truly special times in my
life and remind myself how grateful I am that I found my passion
at a young age. I really hope it will help the reader find theirs.

The first person I'd like to thank for getting this idea off the ground is
Rob Woodhouse, my agent and good friend. To Lucy Oldham and Sara
McMahon at TLA Worldwide, thank you for helping to make sure I was on
track with my writing and had time in my diary to get the book finished
on schedule! Thanks to the fantastic team at The Blair Partnership for
their work in securing the publishing deal and to everyone at Walker
Books, in particular Daisy Jellicoe for all her assistance in
editing and formatting the text.

To Professor Chris Harwood at Loughborough University, who specializes
in sports psychology in youth sport, for his invaluable input and
feedback. To all those people who contributed, whether they realize it
or not, by passing on their knowledge to me over the years and helping
me on my way. To Ray Harris for encouraging me to aim high and have a
plan and to Steve Peters for teaching me how to control my chimp!

To Katarina Johnson-Thompson for her kind words that we used
on the cover, to all my heroes who inspired me to work harder,
and to Steven Spielberg for making the film E.T.!

To my family: my mum, my dad and sister Carrie for their unconditional
love and support that allowed me to follow my dreams. And to my
beautiful wife Sarra for always being there by my side and our amazing
kids, Callum and Chloe, who inspired me to write this book.